THAT'S FOR SURE

Encouragement to Remain in the
One Who Remains with Us

Carrie Ellen

That's For Sure: Encouragement to Remain in the One Who Remains with Us

Shining Roots Publishing
© 2023 by Carrie Ellen
Print Edition

Book Cover Design by ebooklaunch.com
Typeset by: Paul Salvette
Copyediting by: Jessica Snell (jessicasnell.com/editing)

Library of Congress Control Number: 2023911913

ISBN 979-8-218-21684-9 (print)
ISBN 979-8-218-21683-2 (ebook)

To my sons.
You are children of God, you belong to this family,
and I love you very, very much.

Endorsements

Carrie writes with compassion and conviction. She reminds us we are deeply cared for and never alone. *That's For Sure* is overflowing with encouragement and hope.

Bob Goff
New York Times bestselling author
of *Love Does*, *Dream Big*, and
Undistracted

The road beneath our feet can feel awfully rocky these days, and I can't think of a more compassionate and joyful guide than Carrie Ellen. *That's For Sure* will lift your heart and mind, and it will remind you of your true identity in the One who is always sure and always enough.

Kimberly Stuart
Author and podcast host

Through personal storytelling and humor, Carrie encourages us to remain rooted in truth and the promises of God.

Candace, a dependable friend with
power tools and wit

Engaging and thoughtful, Carrie's stories encourage us to consider God's purpose for our lives and to hold fast to his promises.

Tiffany, a sarcastic friend who keeps things real

Carrie's interactions with animals are hilarious. That's not really the point of the book, but you will love reading about how uncomfortable she is near any creature with fur or feathers. You'll laugh and you'll be inspired.

Melinda, a funny friend who brings the laughter to almost every situation

Life is full of ups and downs, twists and turns. *That's For Sure* is a down-to-earth, relatable reminder of the things in this life we can be sure of.

Natalie, a loyal friend who pulls off juggling eighteen thousand different things at any given moment and still gives her people the time of day

Through the perfect pairing of humor and insight, Carrie Ellen paints a beautiful word picture of who God says we are. Wrapped in encouragement and inspiration, you'll be entertained and challenged.

Monique, a friend who's always up for sushi and conversation and who loves a celebratory trip to Disneyland on any given day

Table of Contents

Introduction

A disciple and friend of Jesus named John wrote a letter to his friend Gaius, and in it he said, "I have no greater joy than to hear that my children are walking in the truth."[1] Given what we know about John at this point in his life, he was likely writing about the next generation of believers in Jesus: those younger than him who were walking in the way and truth of Jesus and whom Gaius was likely pastoring at the time.

We also know that this generation was the first who struggled to believe Jesus was both God and man. As you can imagine, this belief caused quite a stir in the culture and in the early church John and Gaius were leading. Part of that early church had become confused about who Jesus was. In turn, this lack of a true and clear picture of Jesus as both God and man had led to confusion about who they were in him.

This could easily describe the world we live in

today. Anytime we lose sight of who Jesus is, in both his fullness and authority as King over all things, and in the sinless life he lived in his humanity, our view of everything else becomes skewed.

As a mom of two boys, I find John's words to Gaius tap into my greatest desire and hope for my sons. Throughout *That's For Sure*, I affectionately refer to my sons as the J Men, and nothing would bring me greater joy than to know they walked through their lives alongside Jesus. I pray they walk out their days in step with the truth of who Jesus is and who he made them to be. I long for them to be rooted in the loving, redemptive story God is writing, to seek Jesus' way above all else, and to walk in step with the movement of the Spirit of God all the days of their lives.

The overflow of this prayer for my sons is the drive behind this book. This is my testimony to them and to you: that abiding in Jesus and remaining kept in who he is, and in who he says we are, is the only way to live. Abiding in him really does bear much fruit, just like he said it would.[2]

Of course I didn't come to this conclusion because life is easy. It's just the opposite, really.

Throughout my lived heartache, disappointment, trials, and fear, Jesus has proved over and over that he is in it with me. He has freely given me his Spirit, who has not once led me astray or caused confusion. He has only ever comforted me, guided me, and helped me.

I know my sons, who are young now, will soon grow to be men and they will square off with hardship, pain, disappointment, trials, and struggles. I simply want to pass on to them what I've come to know to be true about Jesus through some of my own life experiences. I want my testimony of God's faithfulness and care in my life to inspire them to trust and to follow and to obey the God who made them because he loves them.

I've wandered from Jesus and he led me to wonder. I've experienced the depressing depths of disappointment and the nearness of the divine. I have come to know that the creator of the universe not only knows my name, but he also created me to flourish regardless of circumstance. He's proven himself to be my friend—always there, always listening, always speaking truth. This is the testimony I want to leave for my children, for their children, for their children's children and so on.

None of us knows what tomorrow will bring.

But when I read Jesus' words that he is the vine and we are the branches, I am reminded that in him, we are kept. This is his heart for all of us. A healthy branch is nearly impossible to break off of a vine. The branches of a vine are thick and strong—so long as they remain connected to the vine. When connected to the vine, they thrive and produce much fruit.

It is with this understanding and desire that the words in this book are written.

We will begin with the beginning because without knowing our roots and why we were made, life is more confusing than it needs to be. So, we will spend the first section of this book returning to God's design for us and reflecting on his intent for us all. When we look back at the beginning of all things, we find a good and loving God who cares deeply for each one of us.

From there, we will highlight just a few of the gifts Jesus willingly and graciously gives to each one of us to help us survive our days. I share my experiences of coming to know how available Christ is to us, how he came to heal and restore, to offer us friendship like no other, and, finally, his invitation to partner with him in the restoration of all things.

Then we will wrap up the book with a charge to keep going and to walk in step with the Spirit of God, who is always near and whose guiding always leads us in the direction of God's intended plan. As we follow where he leads, we grow in our knowledge of him, we learn to trust him so that we are able to keep on the move with him, and we discover unexplainable joy and hope no matter what may come our way.

That's For Sure is my testimony of the goodness of God in my life. It's my prayer and my charge for the J Men and for each one of us.

May we all walk in the truth and remain kept by the good and loving King Jesus until his glorious return and restoration of all things.

As you read on, I pray you will be encouraged and long for more of Jesus, your creator, protector, friend, and companion.

PART ONE

Rooted in Him

_____

Confession: I am a houseplant lady. I try really hard not to be. I do. But frequent visits to Trader Joe's or Lowe's, with their beautiful green plant displays, do me in every time. The plants practically whisper to me as I walk by, "You need me in your life." I can't argue with their natural variety of bright and rich greens, or with their unique shapes and sizes.

They are right. I do need them. They bring me joy. They add color and life to my home.

I've learned over the years which houseplants are guaranteed to survive under my care and which ones I need to steer clear of if they are to remain healthy and alive.

Take a ZZ plant for example. They are inde-structible. ZZs require very little water and even less attention. They will grow to an impressive height when left absolutely alone. If you so much as side-eye a ZZ plant, you give it anxiety. It's best to let them be and watch them grow. From a distance, of course.

Some of my houseplants have grown so much, I've needed to repot them to create space for them to stretch out and continue to grow. I'm always amazed at the roots of the plants. They are tiny, yet strong. Long, yet coiled. They are wrapped tightly together and impossible to unwind.

Roots give us a visual illustration of God's original design. When roots are well cared for, knit together, and well nourished, the stem and branches are healthy.

When we remain tethered to the God who made us, we flourish.

With roots well cared for and deeply planted, winds may blow and storms may come, yet we remain.

Over the next few chapters, let's peek beneath the soil and remember where we came from and why.

Just like houseplants whisper and ask me to

take them home, God whispers to us the most incredible story ever told. A story saturated in his love for us. A story brimming with care and purpose, and rooted in his goodness.

CHAPTER 1

Who Are You?

A few years ago, Dublin, Ireland, called and I answered. I traveled along with a friend and coworker, Hilary. We were on official business for the pharmaceutical company we worked for at the time. I love traveling and I especially love traveling on the company dime. Working in Ireland didn't feel like work. The food, the people, the accents, the fluffy white sheep, the cows grazing on spacious, green rolling hills—all that I saw and experienced of Ireland was spectacular. I considered not returning to the States, but my husband and our two boys were not on board with that plan.

At one point during our trip, Hilary and I stood on the steps of our hotel next to the bellhop. We were waiting for a cab to whisk us away on our next Irish adventure when a swanky car with dark, tinted windows rolled up along the curb in front of us. A man in a black suit got out of the passenger seat and opened the back door of the car. A balding man with a tiny white mustache stepped out of the car and locked eyes with me. A small entourage of men in black suits quickly surrounded him. He awkwardly kept eye contact with me as he made his way up the stairs of the hotel entrance towards me and Hilary. I noticed an oversized gold medallion hanging around his neck. If you're picturing Flavor Flav, you're not far off.

"Who is this guy and what on the green earth is he wearing?" I muttered under my breath to the bellhop. He smiled and before he had the chance to respond, gold medallion man walked right up to me, extended his hand to shake mine and, with that, asked, "Who are you and where did you come from?"

Well, who are you and where can I pick up some of that obnoxious bling around your neck? Okay, so maybe the men in suits surrounding the guy kept me from spouting off and saying what I was really thinking. Gold medallion man stood tall and proud, firmly gripping my hand in an awkward shake until I answered.

"I'm Carrie and I am from America." I tried

not to be too sarcastic in my tone but I'm certain he could sense cynicism all over my straightforward response. Hilary stood close by, watching the interaction unfold, and tried to hold back laughter. I was so curious who Flavor Flav man was and why he had an entourage surrounding him and his gold medallion.

I bravely continued. "Who are you?" I asked.

I've asked myself the same question many times throughout my life. I'm willing to bet you have too. The quest to know who we are is one that taps into a deep longing of our souls. All of humanity, for all time, shares in this longing to understand who we are, where we came from, and what our purpose is.

How do you answer the who-are-you question?

My first thought is often to respond with what I do for a living or to list one of my titles and talents. I'm a wife, mom, chauffeur, cook, wannabe hip-hop artist, DIYer in training, black-coffee drinker, rule breaker, reader, air drummer extraordinaire. But none of what I do or what you do answers the question of who we are.

I'm in my middle-aged years at this point in my life, and more than ever before, I am fully aware of gravity and how quickly time passes. I pop vitamins now like I did fries in my twenties. When I look in the mirror, I am genuinely shocked by the number of grey hairs sprouting from my little round head. Which can be a bit of a bummer for my two boys, the J Men, because more than a few times now, while out and about with them in tow, I've been mistaken by the general public for their grandma. Sorry, boys. Looking old does have its perks though. Just the other day, cashier Jonathon, at the local Chick-fil-A, took it upon himself to apply the "senior discount" to my order. I wasn't sure if I should've high-fived Jonathon for the discount or karate chopped his throat for assuming I was a senior.

Maybe it's the momma bear in me, or the reality that roughly half of my life is over and I'm realizing just how quickly the past forty-plus years have flown by, but, whatever the reason may be, my soul is tired and grieved over the identity crisis so many are facing today. I'm attempting to navigate this culture and time right alongside you, and so I feel the confusion too. I feel a deep conviction that I should open this first chapter of the book by reminding us of who we are.

And not only of who we are in the depths of our souls, but also of the incredible and carefully crafted purpose for our lives.

I hope to quiet the noise of the anxiety-ridden culture swirling around us and, in its place, help us to, together, zero in on God's perfect design and order, and focus our attention on what he has to say about who we are. And in doing so, I hope to encourage you and to remind you of your very good beginnings and identity.

Out of curiosity, I recently did a Google search for "how to discover my identity'" and "about 426,0000" results popped up. These results just scratch the surface of the issue and are telling of the magnitude of people searching for who they are. We have Google now, but humanity has been searching, one way or another, for who we are and why we have breath in our lungs since time began.

Back in the day, the Greeks poured themselves into matters of academics and rooted their identity in what they knew. Others, such as the Romans during the days when Jesus walked the Earth, found their identity in their ability to conquer a host of foreign peoples and countries. In more recent years, former first lady Nancy Reagan championed the Just Say No to Drugs campaign that swept through schools across America. The goal was to build kids' self-esteem or view of themselves, while also helping them understand the consequences of drug use to the point that they were confidently able to say no to drugs and violence.

These attempts, from the Greeks who based their identity upon knowledge, or the Romans whose identity stemmed from their ability to be victorious over others, to the kids striving to see themselves as valuable through the Just Say No movement, have all failed in their attempts to answer our universal longing to know who we are. Looking to ourselves and our own abilities will not help us discover who we are. Our compass of truth must extend beyond our own understanding if we are to fully grasp and live into the fullness of who we were created to be.

I want to encourage you—and I need this encouragement right alongside you—that who we are and why we're here has already been determined and appointed. The pressure is off, friend. You and I do not have to search for who we are and for meaning in this life. We need only to fix our eyes upon the good and loving God who fashioned us into his likeness long ago and who spoke us into being out of his great love. With eyes fixed upon him and seeing him as he truly is, we begin to better understand and see in ourselves who he made us to be. Looking upon him is like looking into a mirror. In the same way we see a reflection of ourselves as we look into a mirror, when we look at God and who he is, we see the reflection of his goodness upon us.

I mentioned I'm a mom to the J Men. They haven't reached the ages yet where they are totally embarrassed by me, although lately the eye rolls of the oldest J Man tell me the embarrassment season is quickly approaching. As their mom, I want my boys to be confident in who God created them to be. I long for this because I know if there's any confusion or doubt about who made them and why they have breath in their lungs, they will stumble along in every area of their lives, without solid footing under their feet.

In an effort to keep them rooted in the identity God gave them, I tell my boys a simple truth. Every day, before they leave the house, I say to them, "You are a child of God. You belong to this family and I love you very much." My hope is this phrase will serve as a building block in their childhood, so that when life gets really hard and really confusing (because it will), they will hear their grandma-looking momma reminding them of who they are and the goodness God has created them with. In this way, I hope they keep their gaze fixed upon God and trust his Word declaring them to be "very good"[1] above all other voices, even if hearing their momma say these words in some seasons of their childhood embarrasses them.

In the brilliant book *Name Above All Names*[2], coauthored by friends and pastors Alistair Begg and Sinclair B. Ferguson, we are reminded that, for the follower of Jesus and child of God, we see not with our eyes, but with our ears. It's the Word of God, and his Word alone, that, when heard, when obeyed, when trusted and followed, runs deep into our hearts and souls and declares who we are. The Word of God tethers us to our Creator so that no matter how great the pull towards anything other than God and his Word may be, we remain.

Knowing who we are and living a life to the fullest of God's intent is defined by his Word. What it's not defined by is the temporal things of this world, such as knowledge, fleeting jobs, relationships, titles and fame, or the circumstances we see surrounding us.

My friend Candace helped me see this in a new way a few years back. Candace and her kids went to the beach with me and the J Men one afternoon.

I sat on a beach towel and watched Candace, down by the water, take the oldest J Man by the hand. She showed him how to dig his heels deep into the wet sand. As the waves broke before them, they stood firmly planted in the sand. The waters rushed up and hugged them at the knees and they stood still.

I once dug my heels into my degrees and my life experiences, and it drove me straight to Miserableville faster than two shakes of a lamb's tail. I had planted roots in the shifting sand of insecurity and pride. My eyes were focused on my accolades and what I had accomplished. My vision was skewed and, because of it, I forgot the truth I had heard. I relied on myself to stand firm and when the waves hit, I crashed upon the shore right along with them.

In his grace and mercy—and not without growing pains and roundhouse kicks to my pride—Jesus taught me to dig my heels into him and into what he says is true and eternal.

He made you and me to be people who see with our ears. It's the superpower of the Jesus follower. We trust in what we've heard, not in what we see.

My son, standing hand in hand with Candace,

saw the waves coming, but he did not panic, turn, and run away. Instead, he trusted her and what she had told him about digging his heels into the sand, and he stood firm as the waves crashed before him. Watching Candace stand next to my oldest J man gave me the sweetest picture of what it looks like for Jesus to stand with us, shoulder to shoulder, heels dug deep into his Word, through all life's circumstances. It reminds me to trust his Word regardless of what my eyes may see.

Throughout life, a lot of things will come before us that are pleasing to our eye. But these things are fleeting and will not last. The Word of God will last for eternity. As we place our trust in what we hear from God and what we read in the Bible, all that is true will come into focus. His Word is the anchor we so desperately need to keep our footing throughout the struggles of this life.

Jesus never intended for you and me to feel the weight and pressure to identify and define who we are to the world around us. He knows the longing in our hearts to understand and live into who we are because he created us to find the answer to that longing in him and who he says we are.

The best news ever is that he's already defined, named, and claimed who we are. We need only to take a deep breath and look to him. In him, we will not only see and discover who we are, but he will cement our feet upon solid, unshakable ground we can be sure of. He's designed and created a way of life that sets us free from feeling the pressure to come up with our best guess as to who we are. We don't need a Google search engine to help us discover our identity and purpose.

Jesus' brother James reminds us that "every good and perfect gift is from above, coming down from the Father of the heavenly lights, who does not change like shifting shadows."[3]

In other words, God is the source of all good things in life. Contentment, security and identity, affirmation, and every good and perfect gift is from him. And thankfully, he doesn't change his mind like we change socks.

If you've been using your eyes to search for someone or something around you to help you decide who you are, rest easy, friend. The pressure is off. There's no need to look further than the Bible on your nightstand. Open it up, point your finger at a verse on a page, and start there. Read the Word. Open your ears to what God says is true. In it, you'll discover your superpower to see with your ears, not your eyes.

And then take a nap. You can rest in assurance of God's good design for your life.

With feet burrowed deep into what Jesus says is true, you will be held up and sustained by him as waves of life come crashing in around you. And they will come. Nothing is wasted with Jesus. When you let him, he will use the crashing waves to draw you nearer and nearer to him.

He can be trusted because he is the author of your life. "He is before all things, and in him all things hold together."[4] He is the way, the truth, and the life.[5] He created you, formed you, redeemed you. He calls you by name and he walks with you.[6]

Even when you don't feel sure and your eyes deceive you, you can bank on the words of the God who formed you and calls you his own.

I recently had to surrender my California state driver's license because I'm now a resident of Texas, y'all.

Handing over my license was a strange experience. In exchange, I received a piece of paper, a temporary Texas driver's license. But does holding a Texas driver's license make me any less a California girl? Not really. I'm still Carrie from California. I still wear Rainbow sandals when it's cold outside.

I'm no less a Californian now that I've taken up residence in Texas.

The same is true for the believer in Jesus. Our identity is wrapped up in who God says we are, not in the zip code or the culture we find ourselves in today.

Identity comes from the Creator, not a card. And it is not in what or who we know, what we've accomplished, or even what we think of ourselves.

No matter what your current circumstances are, or what you see in front of you with your eyes, trust the voice of the one who made you above all else.

The one who formed you is the only one who can truly inform you of who you are.

And you are exactly who Jesus says you are. You were carefully and beautifully designed and brought into existence by his hand. You are and have all you'll ever need because he crafted your life for a perfect purpose.

Slap that truth on an ID card or on a medallion around your neck and live your life with heels deeply dug into the Word that does not change. It's who you are.

With ears bent towards God's Word, we discover who we are.

The medallion-wearing Irishman did let me in on who he was. He was the then Lord Mayor of Dublin, Nial Ring. You can look him up online and see his bling and tiny white mustache. He was very kind and I have no idea why the Lord Mayor of Dublin beelined it to me and asked me who I was. But I'll take it as an opportunity to be reminded that I am a child of God, I belong to his family, and he loves me very much. And with that understanding and foundation laid, all else falls into place.

And, let me remind you as well, friend, you are a child of God, you belong to his family, and he loves you very much!

That's for sure.

CHAPTER 2

The Song and the Story

I once worked at a church as the outreach pastor. While that role took me into the community most of the week, on Sundays I often helped with the services by bringing a word of encouragement during the worship set.

It was a typical Sunday morning. I took my cue—the slight head nod in my direction from the worship pastor—and I went up on the stage. I made sure my handheld microphone was on and I greeted the congregation. "Good morning, everyone! My name is Carrie and I serve as the worship pastor here." I continued my spiel, completely unaware of my word slip, wrapped it up, and handed things back over to the actual worship pastor. When I got back to my seat in the front row next to the lead pastor and his wife, the lead pastor leaned over, laughing, and said, "Do you realize you just introduced yourself as the worship pastor?"

I had no idea. It was a good thing everyone else had already moved on to loudly singing another song, because I was laughing hysterically. The shoulder-shaking, mouth-open-but-no-sound-coming-out, bent-over, hands-on-knees, tears-streaming-down-hot-cheeks kind of laughter. I laughed at the thought of how confusing it must have been for guests that day to see the worship pastor onstage next to the crazy lady who introduced herself as the worship pastor. I laughed at the thought of how those who knew me who were likely having their own laughs because they knew I misspoke. And finally, I gut laughed at the absurdity of me claiming to be a worship pastor on a Sunday morning.

I can't carry a tune any more than I can carry a piano.

But although I could never be a worship pastor or lead anyone in a song without making ears bleed, glass break, dogs howl, and babies cry, I've got a song in my heart. I believe you do too.

I believe you and I are wired with a song to sing simply as a reflection of the one who created us.

In chapter one, we touched ever so briefly on the idea that God made us and our identity is wrapped up in who he says we are. In this chapter, we will dig a bit deeper into why he made us and why it matters.

God is actively writing a story and a song that you and I are part of. God has been writing this incredible story and song since the beginning of time. We need to start at the beginning of the story to understand the setting we find ourselves in today, because without a clear view of the beginning, our present view is warped. If we lack a solid foundation beneath our feet, consisting of knowledge of who we are and God's intention for us in this world, we can live our entire lives feeling like we're in a constant state of being late to the party.

It's in the beginning of all things that we learn who God is, what he's like, and what his intentions behind creating us were—and continue to be today.

I was once late to the movies with my friend Jamie. She and I had stopped for burritos, as you do, and we walked into the theater ten minutes late to see the 2004 release *Napoleon Dynamite*. Judging by the setting and style portrayed in the movie, Jamie and I assumed it took place in the 1980s. Given the cars, the Caboodles, the puffy sleeves, the high school lockers, and the Hammer pants throughout the movie, we thought we were watching a storyline that took place twenty years earlier.

Jamie and I loved the movie and returned the very next night to see it again. Okay, so maybe we were avoiding our graduate studies like the plague. However, this time, we got there in time to see the opening scene. As the introduction flashed Napoleon's high school ID card up on the screen, we noticed the school year displayed was not from the 1980s. It was the current year. We looked at each other in shock and cracked up. The movie had been hilarious under our assumption that it took place in the 80s and now that we had realized it was modern-day, it became that much funnier.

In every story, be it a book or a movie, our perspective of the middle is fuzzy and incomplete without the framework of the opening scene. If we miss the introduction of a story, we simply cannot make sense of what's before us.

Beginnings matter. The beginning of the world matters. The God who spoke it into existence matters. Your beginning matters.

Thankfully, one of the many good gifts God has given us is the gift of letting us in on the beginning of the world. Having the story of the beginning helps us to rightly understand what he had in mind for all of creation; yes, that means you too. Clear and right understanding of how all things began, and why they began at all, helps us to see and know that all God made is good. And this understanding helps us stay connected to him and to see him all around us and in every circumstance.

Of the many creation theories, my absolute favorite is the idea that God sang creation into existence as an expression of his love for all he made. Genesis 1 certainly resembles the liturgical makeup of a song. In God's creation song, the act of creating is the verses and his reflection about all he's made—"it is good"—is the chorus.

He was orderly and worked in harmony with his Spirit and Jesus. Yes, Jesus was there too. We see the Trinity working together in the first three verses of the Bible. In the beginning, God created, the Spirit of God hovered, and the Word spoke creation into existence.

The disciple John would later refer to the "Word" as he told his account of Jesus' birth on the Earth. "In the beginning was the Word, and the Word was with God, and the Word was God. He was with God in the beginning."[1]

At the end of the final day of creation, the day he made man in his image, he "saw all that he had made, and it was very good."[2] Pause for just a moment here and imagine God singing you into existence. God saw [insert your name] and called you very good.

Job, an ancient story found in the Bible, affirms the idea that God sang creation into existence. Not only that, but creation responded with singing back to God.[3] Job described the original call and response.

As a mom, I find it surprisingly easy to literally burst into song at the mere sight of my sons. I cannot set a plate of food in front of them without singing "your dinner is reeaddyy!" When they were babies, I would sing "it's bath time" as I got them ready to clean the day's dirt and grime off. (If you read "it's bath time" to the tune of M. C. Hammer's famous hit "U Can't Touch This," we just became fast friends.).

Singing is a way for us to express our deepest emotions when merely speaking words simply doesn't go far enough. We sing to express our felt emotions such as joy, sorrow, gratitude, delight, pain, suffering, and every emotion in between. Singing is the cry of our heart.

This idea that God sang creation into existence feels a lot like a personal invitation and a beckoning from him to us to glimpse his heart—to know him and to know what he cares most about.

I wonder if the song of God's heart sounds like the constant display of his love poured out over all creation. The rising and setting of the sun, the waves crashing along the shore, the rustling of the oak-tree leaves in the wind, the attention-commanding height of the redwoods, the budding tulips in the spring, the chirping of birds at the earliest morning light.

What if God, in his overwhelming love for all creation, sang all things into existence? What if creation is the song of his heart? What if our lives reflect the truth that God sang us into existence from a posture of overflowing love? What if this is our beginning? If we believed this were true, would we live our lives differently? What if he delights in us so much that he is ever present, ever caring, endlessly loving, and rejoicing over us with a constant song every day of our lives?

I love how Sally Lloyd-Jones, author of *The Jesus Storybook Bible*, illustrates the love of God at creation:

> God wrote, "I love you"—he wrote it in the sky, and on the earth, and under the sea. He wrote his message everywhere! Because God created everything in his world to reflect him like a mirror—to show us what he is like, to help us know him, to make our hearts sing!
>
> …The way red poppies grow wild. The way a dolphin swims.
>
> And God put it into words, and wrote it in a book called "the Bible."[4]

There's a line in there about a cat too, but since I am not a fan of the furry felines, I left that part out.

However, I really do love the part about how knowing God makes our hearts sing. And to think this is how everything, included you and me, began: with bubbling-up-and-over love and song from God, the Creator of all living things. This is the most wonderful, unexpected, joyful beginning.

Recognizing and believing that this is the truth we've been designed for deeply impacts how we see ourselves and those around us. As individuals with our unique differences, God created all of us out of an abundance of song and love when he meticulously designed us. Creation isn't something that simply happened a long time ago that we are far removed from today.

Rather, the God who created the world with order and delight created us with the same attention to detail, artistry, and care. His love bubbled over then as sky, light, mountains, and oceans formed and his love continues to bubble up and over and with the kind of love that makes God sing over our lives here and now.

With so much noise, distraction, and chaos around us at any given moment, it is easy to forget our roots. We can easily get caught up in the hustle and bustle of life and lose all sight of the truth of where we've come from and the eternal hope of where we are going.

However, no matter how difficult or trying our circumstances may be or may become, the truth of God's loving design for us is unchanging, unwavering, and unmoving. God and his unshakable, loving ways have not changed since the very beginning.

God's desire for us to know him runs deep—so deep that super-smart scholars who have studied the name God gave to himself, YHWH, believe his name to be the very breath we breathe. (Sandra Thurman Caporale, from the Memorial Church of Christ in Houston, authored a blog that captures this imagery beautifully.[5])

Inhale.

Exhale.

Can you hear his name as you breathe? We have been meticulously and intentionally made by a good God who calls us his own. He delights in us. He sings a happy song over our lives. He longs to be close to us and so he put his name on our breath to constantly remind us of his goodness and love.

With eyes wide open to the goodness of God, we will see him everywhere.

I was reminded of this not too long ago when I witnessed a solar eclipse. If you've had the opportunity to see one, you know you need to be well equipped with viewing glasses, paper plates, and cardboard boxes to take in the glory and wonder of it all without damaging your precious little eyeballs.

I witnessed the solar eclipse from the top deck of a parking structure near where I worked at the time. Through my special viewing glasses, I watched the moon align with the sun. It was an incredible sight. I was reminded of how purposeful and intricately detailed God is with creation.

David put words to my thoughts: "When I consider your heavens, the work of your fingers, the moon and the stars, which you have set in place, what is mankind that you are mindful of them?"[6]

The eclipse proved to be an incredible display of God's design, creativity, and glory. And, as beautiful as it was, God's greatest display of design, creativity, and glory was actually not up in the sky—it was standing all around me in the form of the dozens of other people watching from the deck of the parking structure that day. People are God's most magnificent creation. You and I are the crown of his glory.

As wonderful as the sun and moon are, you are the workmanship of God. You bear his image. You breathe his name. You were created on purpose, and for a purpose only you can fulfill. In those moments when life is hard and you feel down, look up, and let the sun and the moon serve as a reminder of not only who you are, but whose you are.

You bear his fingerprint! You belong to his family. He chose you! His glory is displayed best to the world not through special viewing glasses, but rather, through love—love for God and love for others.

I was late to the movies once, but you are not late to your life. You are right where you need to be today. God created all things from a place of incredible love. The kind of love that makes his heart sing. He made you to know him so that your heart can sing too. You reflect his goodness and when he made you, he called you *very good*. His name is declared on your very breath. Yes, even on the days when your breath is rancid (you know you have those days), his goodness never departs.

He is with you. He saves. He delights in you. His joy in you is so great, he bursts into song at the mere thought of you.

When you're struggling to find your song, go to the one who sings over you with joy and gladness. Read his words. He will hold you up and give you strength to press on.

With all the uncertainty swirling around, the one thing you can be sure of is that God created you out of his love for you and that's worth singing about, even if you sing off-key like me. Find your song and belt it. It's okay if you're in a quiet coffee shop or at the library; sing it out! The world needs to experience more expression of God's love, so don't hold back. Sing it like you're the worship pastor on a Sunday morning—even if you're not.

Your story reflects the greatest story ever told—the story with the incredible beginning.

You are the result of God's love and part of his eternal song and story.

You were thought of and so deeply loved by God before you even took your first breath.

You were made strong and courageous. You were made with careful design and dignity.

You are God's very good design! And he is with you today.

That's for sure.

CHAPTER 3

Protected

Several years ago, I visited Romania with a small group from church. After a drive through the gorgeous green rolling Transylvania hills and the breathtakingly beautiful Carpathian Mountains, we stopped to visit an ancient fortress made entirely from stone and built in 1300 AD. In its day, it was unconquerable, and even so many centuries later, its stone walls were still standing. The fortress, which had a long bridge as its entrance, was square in shape, with four towering stone walls to defend each side. Finally, a large round watchtower stood tall within the walls of the fortress.

I explored the thousand-year-old structure like a kid on a playground. I climbed the stone walls and made my way up to the highest points. The fortress, nestled between beautiful green rolling hills, had once protected a community of people from attack. It was their defense against harm. It was their security. It surrounded them by high walls and protected them from the dangers of the outside world.

Experiencing the fortress gave me fresh perspective on the psalmist's words, "The LORD is my rock, my fortress and my deliverer; my God is my rock, in whom I take refuge, my shield and the horn of my salvation, my stronghold."[1]

Admitting we need protection is never easy. Relying on and trusting another for what we think we can achieve or obtain on our own is about as tough as thousand-year-old stone.

And yet, it is the loving characteristic of God to protect, surround, and defend me and you. In chapter two, we focused our time on the truth that God created us and all living things out of goodness and love. And God didn't stop with simply creating us. He didn't speak you and me into existence, push us out into the world, and say, "Good luck out there. Let's hope for the best." That would be cruel and not at all reflective of his kindness and care.

Rather, God went on to create a home for mankind, as recorded in Genesis 2. We know it today as the Garden of Eden. I can be a bit of a word nerd at times, so I did a little digging into the Hebrew word for garden, which is *ganan*[2]. Ganan means to "cover, surround, defend." It can also be defined as the hidden place—a place completely wrapped up and hidden in the goodness and care of the creator, something like a fortress.

Jesus is the caretaker of the garden, that is, the gardener, the one whose very nature protects, defends, and surrounds those whom he loves. Furthermore, Eden means to delight. In simple terms—for simple minds like mine—what we're saying here is that it delights Jesus beyond what we may ever understand to be your protection, your defense, and to surround you with his love and care.

Jesus is our fortress. You were made to be kept by him, to stick near him, to look to him in all circumstances of your life, and to depend solely upon him.

This is easier said than done, I know. If we're bent towards anything, it's fending for ourselves. We've had to depend on ourselves to survive the day, the hard thing, the difficult person, and so on. In an effort to be our own protectors of our world, we inevitably, and often inadvertently, hide. We isolate. We take a step back and build walls to keep ourselves protected from anything or anyone who may see our struggles and strife.

We see this happen with Adam and Eve the moment they eat the forbidden fruit. They had a choice to make. They could have run to God and explained what had happened and looked to him to be their helper. But they didn't. Instead, they looked to themselves, felt shame, and hid.

They traded dependence upon God for independence from him, and it cost them—and us—our confidence in God's defense and love of us.

However, as mentioned in the last chapter, nothing surprises God. Nothing catches him off guard. He knew we would struggle to depend upon him for all things, and Adam and Eve's decision didn't thwart God's plan for them to remain hidden in him.

In an unexpected act of mercy, love, and protection, God made clothes for Adam and Eve, to cover them. Even though they did exactly what he told them not to do, God loved them and protected them through it.

God hasn't changed. He still extends mercy and protection. His protection over you is illustrated by how he rescues, redeems, and renews. Jesus shows up in our darkest hour to draw us near to him, because it's proximity to him that brings protection and peace, despite circumstance.

I don't know about you, but when I go about my life, doing what I think is best for me, I inevitably find myself isolated and without protection. I'm like my own private island, but with nothing and no one around as a defense. How quickly I can fall into the lie that makes me think I can fix and solve my problems on my own! I believe this is what Adam and Eve must has felt when they hid from God. Yet this is in complete opposition to what God intends for us. You and I were not made to hide from him, rather, we were made to hide *in* him.

My sons, the J Men, teach me all the time what it looks like to stick close to Jesus and to look to him as our protector and defender throughout all of life. I constantly see them protecting each other—especially the oldest J Man, who constantly looks out for youngest J Man. The oldest J Man is hyperaware of the need to look out for his brother. When in a parking lot, he instinctively reaches for Little J Man's hand. He doesn't wave a sword at the danger of cars passing by, pulling in and out of parking stalls; he simply holds Little J Man's hand

and pulls him in tight, right by his side. Proximity to his brother, hand in hand, is how he protects.

Jesus shows up with his protecter/gardener hat on all throughout Scripture. For Noah and his family and the animals, the Lord's protection was the ark, or *teba*[3] in Hebrew. The ark was an instrument of salvation that Jesus used to protect and save Noah, his family, and the animals from the flood.

The word teba is used only one other time in all of Scripture. It's the word used for the cradle little baby Moses was placed in when his mom and sister Miriam crafted a plan to save his life from certain death under the hand of an evil pharaoh.

Noah's ark protected and saved Noah and his family from the flood. Moses' cradle protected and saved him, and thereby saved the nation of Israel, a foreshadowing of the protection and salvation Jesus—born in a manger, not unlike a cradle— would bring to the whole world.

You may recall a detail that is easy to overlook in the story of Mary Magdalene when she found the tomb of Jesus empty on the third day after his death. Startled because his body was missing from the tomb, Mary saw a man who she, at first glance, thought was the gardener. But mere moments later, Jesus would say her name and she would be the first to see the resurrected Lord Jesus.

I wonder if she knew then that she had indeed seen *the gardener*—the one whose very purpose is to defend God's people, to protect them, and to surround them with his unchanging love. Sometimes the best of things can come from someone believing they made a mistake, like the mistake that led to the glorious invention of French fries. Mary thought she got it wrong at first glance, but boy oh boy, did her mistaken identity of Jesus prove to be more real than she likely even imagined possible.

By his resurrection, Jesus, the Gardener, has made a way for Mary and all of humanity forevermore to once again be near him, hidden in him, well within his protection and defense. He restored all that was lost in the Garden of Eden. We may not live in the Garden of Eden today, but because the Gardener lives, we can certainly know his protection and we can live surrounded and defended by his unending love, mercy, and grace today. In this very moment, he is our fortress.

When my life felt chaotic during the 2007 recession, I struggled to find work, the debt of student loans piled high, and anxiety and stress took over. I watched my hopes of what life after school would be like wash away and a new reality of the unknown set it. I felt alone and abandoned by God. I was in a season of looking to myself for answers and help. I had forgotten that I am never alone and left to figure out life on my own. I had forgotten that he was my protector and I had nothing to fear.

But God, in his mercy, reminded me that his plan established long ago in the Garden of Eden was still a good plan. When I feel distant from God, as we all will do at times, I remember the stories throughout the biblical narrative of how he's shown up for so many others. These stories are his gift to us. When I need protection, I know I can run to him. I can hide *in* him and not away *from* him.

When your expectations don't come to pass like you wanted, remember God designed you to find your security in him. When you fail at something you want so badly, don't keep it from him. Take it to him and spill your guts out before him.

Life is hard. Jesus can handle it. Not only can Jesus handle your cares and burdens, it brings him absolute joy to do so. Go to him in all things, and he will protect you, defend you, and surround you with his love, and he'll do it all with joy and gladness.

He sees the struggle you're in right now. He knows the opposition you're up against as you seek to live righteously in an unrighteous society. And just like God remembered Noah in his day, he will remember you too. He seeks to protect and to save you. He may not take you completely out of the struggle you're in, but he is with you every step of the way through it.

God remembered me during the recession. And because not a single thing is wasted with God, he used the hardship of that season to draw me so close to him.

When the future of a flood seemed so unreal and no doubt scary, Noah hammered away anyway, believing God was with him. Pound your nails into the truth of who God is today. When life's struggles hit, you'll know he is with you, and he remembers you! He is your fortress. You will find rest, security, and salvation in him.

You don't have to go all the way to Romania and experience a man-made fortress in order to understand this truth. Simply talk to Jesus wherever you are and about whatever you're going through, and watch him show up to protect you, surround you, and defend you. He cares for you.

His shield is safe.

We're going to end this chapter by reflecting on Psalm 91. While scholars are not certain, it is widely believed Moses may have written this poetic and truth-filled psalm. Moses was kept alive because of that tiny cradle—teba—he was placed in as a baby. His life was full of hardship and time after time he was faced with the decision to trust God and remain hidden in him or trust himself and do what he thought was right, which would have resulted in isolation.

Not much has changed since then. We face the same choices today. Psalm 91 is a wonderful reminder of God, and of his protecting love that we can be absolutely sure of throughout all that comes our way. You can trust the Gardener, who made the way for you to experience his love and protection even in this dangerous life.

I hope you will read through the psalm on your own as you have time. But for our purposes here, I'm simply going to highlight all the Lord does for those who remain hidden in him. Let these truths wash over you anew today. After all, God designed you to be by his side in all things, protected and defended by him, and surrounded by his love.

He who dwells in the shelter of the Most High will find rest.

He is my shelter; my fortress. I can trust him.

He will save me.

He will cover me.

I will find refuge.

His faithfulness is my shield.

I will not fear.

No harm will find me because you are my refuge.

You command your angels to guard me.

Because you love me, you will rescue me.

You protect me.

When I call upon you, you answer me.

You are with me in my time of need.

You deliver me and honor me.

You give life and salvation.

That's for sure.

CHAPTER 4

Family Business

During my college years, I spent most of my time learning to tame my frizzy hair and keep my unibrow in check. Until I met Holiday. Holiday was a guest speaker in my human service class. She shared about the many families living in motels along the boulevards near the school campus. I had grown up in the area and it had never occurred to me that so many called the motels home. Holiday had created a nonprofit organization that existed to befriend and build relationships with one particular motel's residents. She called it Miracles-In-Motion.

Upon my college graduation, Holiday kindly offered me a job as a coordinator with the non-profit. For over two years, I spent my days engaging with those who called the motel home. Some days were filled with fun and joy, while others overwhelmed me with sadness, pain, and trauma. I saw firsthand the vicious cycle of husbands and fathers being in jail, then returning home, and then ending up in jail again. I witnessed the destructive power of domestic abuse. I remember the day a teen boy returned home from school and found that his mom had taken her life in their shared motel room.

Days were hard at the motel.

Miracles-In-Motion proved to be a little ray of sunshine around the motel. Volunteers from the church that the organization was associated with began to show up consistently to spend time with the residents. Their presence alone showed the men and woman at the motel that someone saw them, cared for them, and that they mattered. They often brought balls to kick around with the kids and nail polish for the girls to do their nails with and sidewalk chalk for all the children to play with.

Church ladies brought pizza and cupcakes just because. Thank goodness it was pizza and not church-lady casseroles. Can I get a witness?

Everything we've been talking about in the chapters leading up to this one—who we are, how we came to be, and what Jesus is up to as rescuer, protector, and redeemer—seemed to collide at the motel. Many of the residents I grew to know and love had lost their true identity and God-given dignity somewhere along the way. And for a sea of different reasons.

One sweet family of five lost all they had, their business and home, when medical bills and a cancer diagnosis overwhelmed them. Others lost their jobs and struggled to find work again. Many had disabilities that made working a nine-to-five job nearly impossible. The reason people ended up at the motel varied, but all had a common thread of reality they faced.

Broken relationships with estranged family members were a broken-record story that wove its way in and out of the motel.

When the cancer diagnosis came, when the layoff came, when the financial struggle hit, they only had themselves to rely on. Broken relationships with family members left them isolated, and in times when they desperately needed the support of others, they had no one to ask for help.

Feelings of isolation aren't limited to motels. I often feel the pull to isolate myself when I'm overwhelmed by a situation. I think we all do. Most of the time this comes from a place of good intention. We don't set out to isolate ourselves from those around us, be it family or friends. I think we just don't want to bother anyone or become a burden to those around us.

It's no help at all that our American culture is very individualistic. We hear all the time that our destiny is up to us. The "American dream" is rooted in this ideology. Work hard and you'll reap the benefits. Nothing in that messaging is community oriented or focused. And while there is nothing wrong with working hard and being rewarded for it, this idea causes us to believe we don't need help from anyone, not even our own families.

But as we've seen in the chapters leading up to this, in no way were we made to depend solely upon ourselves. This twisted and false idea came into play only after Adam and Eve fell prey to the lie that suggested that if they ate the forbidden fruit, they would be like God and, therefore, no longer need him like they once did.

The motel was such a tangible picture of the devastation this trickery has caused. But Jesus has overwhelming compassion upon his people. During my time with Miracles-In-Motion, I experienced Jesus, the Gardener, protect, defend, and surround those who were hurting and isolated. I witnessed firsthand the power of community in people's lives. I saw hope returned to those who had lost all hope. I saw once-estranged families reunite and grow supportive of each other.

And to get there, in every case, someone had to be willing—and brave enough—to interrupt a family member or friend they knew who might be able help them. And then that same someone had to be vulnerable enough to ask for the help.

We learn as kids not to interrupt. It's rude, our parents said. When the adults are talking, kids wait. What I find so interesting when I read about Jesus is how often people got healed because Jesus allowed for an interruption. We see it throughout the gospel books of the Bible, beginning with the very first recorded miracle. Jesus was enjoying a wedding celebration, likely busting a move on the dance floor, as you do, when his mom interrupted him and asked him to do something to keep the wine flowing and the party happening.

Then there's the time when Jesus was in a home, chatting up the crowds, teaching them about his ways, and someone interrupted him by digging a hole in the roof and lowering a paralytic down at Jesus' feet.

I don't know the exact number of times Jesus

allowed for an interruption so that he could bring healing to someone, but I'm pretty sure it's in the gazillions.

A personal favorite interruption-turned-healing story of mine was written by a guy named Luke. Luke was a doctor and a great storyteller. Luke gives us the inside scoop on an action-packed day when Jesus healed two people who could not have been more different—not unlike those who lived in the motel and those who volunteered at the motel.

We find the story in Luke 8. The first person, Jairus, was a church leader and well respected in the community. The second person, a bleeding woman, who isn't given a name in the Bible, was an outcast.

Because of the illness that plagued her with uncontrollable bleeding, and due to Jewish customs in her day, she was forced to live outside the city walls. Her bleeding illness labeled her as unclean, unwelcome, and unwanted in her community. Desperate for healing, she had spent all she had on doctors' visits to no avail. She was poor and alone.

Jairus' daughter was dying. Desperate for help, Jairus boldly asked Jesus to heal his daughter and to do it now, before it was too late. As Jesus was on his way to Jairus' house, a large crowd of looky-loos formed, hoping to catch a glimpse of a miracle taking place. The crowds pressed in on Jesus and the disciples did their best to play bodyguard, circling him up in protection as he hurried off towards Jairus' house.

But the bleeding woman, in a bold and daring move, slipped through the crowds and managed to touch just the hem of the clothes Jesus wore. Instantly, her bleeding stopped.

And so did Jesus.

Interruption.

Jesus turned and asked, "Who touched me?" You can imagine the shock on everyone's faces. With such a large crowd around Jesus, anyone could have touched him. We don't know what Jairus was doing or thinking when Jesus stopped, but I highly doubt he remained calm as he realized Jesus was standing still while his daughter's life still hung in the balance. When no one answered Jesus the first time, he patiently reiterated that someone had touched him. He also let it be known that healing power had gone out from him.

Finally, the bleeding woman identified herself as the one who had touched him.

It's striking that Jesus stopped for the unseen

and unwanted nuisance in the crowd.

The story would've been great had it ended there. It would've gone down as another miracle by Jesus. Just one more allowed interruption turned into healing. He could've sent her on her way now that her bleeding stopped, and continued to Jairus' house to attend to a dying girl.

But Jesus rolls a little differently than we expect. What did he do? He gave her space to share her story.

Listen, after twelve years in isolation, enduring poverty, chronic pain, and suffering, I imagine she gave Jesus and the onlooking crowd an earful. We don't know how long it took Chatty Cathy to convey her story to Jesus, but we know he allowed for her interruption, despite being on his way to a life-and-death situation at Jairus' house.

Jesus' response to hearing her story is even more radical than his healing of her physical body. He called her "daughter." The woman who doesn't get a name in the Bible and who was considered an outsider, a nobody, was now family to Jesus. The outsider became the insider. He took the time to turn towards her, look upon her with compassion, and listen to her story. He saw her for who she really was: his daughter, created in his image and designed to reflect his goodness to those around her.

To be seen and known as who God designed you and me to be—his children—is what it means to be truly healed.

Healing is personal to Jesus. This was a family matter. She was his daughter. She was suffering and he did something about it. By allowing the interruption and giving her space to unleash her grievances, he restored his relationship with her and he healed her soul.

The story only gets more nail-biting as we learn Jairus' daughter died waiting on Jesus to arrive. But I'll leave that part of the story for you to read on your own. Pop some popcorn and sit awhile in the entire story.[1] It's a good one.

We aren't told what happened to the daughter after her encounter with Jesus, but I think it's safe to say she went back to her people, her family, her community. It's not difficult to imagine she may have lived the remainder of her days with an open-door policy in place. I'm willing to bet my beloved houseplants, Hank and Flow, that she was okay with allowing for interruptions by others for the rest of her life. I imagine the healing she experienced through restored community—first with

Jesus and then with her family—extended to so many others as she made space for them and reminded them of the truth of who they were.

Jesus' heart for his people is not contingent upon zip codes or statuses. He's concerned with healing the hurting. He desires to restore all things, namely me and you, back to our hidden place in the family of God. He doesn't see people who live in a motel any differently than he sees those who live in a palace. He does see hurt, pain, suffering, physical poverty, and poverty of the heart, and he longs to restore us to the way he intended us to be in the Garden of Eden.

—————

I've often wondered how the story in Luke may have been different had all the spectators who crowded in on Jesus had enough faith to stop him in his tracks, believing he could and would heal them too. How often do we sit on the sidelines, watching Jesus do his thing in the lives of others while we wait, unsure he'll do the thing for us?

So many things keep us on the bench instead of

in the game. Fear of being exposed. Shame for past mistakes. Feeling like our problems are so small compared to others' and, frankly, feeling like Jesus has more important things to do. We're afraid to interrupt Jesus for dozens of reasons. Had the crowd pressing in on Jesus met him with their need like Jairus and the bleeding woman did, I believe Jesus would've taken all the time needed to stop, turn towards, listen to, and heal every person in his path that day.

There's a Hebrew word for this personal healing Jesus did throughout his earthly ministry and continues to do today. The word is *gâ'al* and it refers to the act of redemption.[2] The *go'el* is the one who redeems.

Theologian Christopher J. H. Wright explains, "A go'el was any member within a wider family group upon whom fell the duty of acting to protect the interests of the family or another member in it who was in particular need. The term might be translated, "'kinsman protector' or 'family champion.'"[3]

Healing is Jesus' family business. The state of your soul is a very personal family matter to him. God cares so deeply for you and me that he sent Jesus on a mission to rescue us from all the pain and hurt we carry throughout our lives.

There are three qualifications of a go'el that must come into play if redemption is to take place. First, the redeemer must be near to those in need of redemption. Second, he must be able to redeem, and, finally, he must be willing to redeem.

Jesus showed us his desire to be near by leaving heaven's glory and willingly humbling himself to enter our broken world as a baby. And he lived a completely human life. He got hungry. He got tired. He limited himself to space and time—all out of a longing to be near his people. Jesus has authority over all things. Therefore, he is able to redeem all things. And finally, he is willing.

His willingness to redeem is the clincher for me. While we were in our desperate need, he willingly went to the cross, suffered, and died in order to redeem us through his resurrection. The Bible also tells us it brought him joy to take on the cross on our behalf, because by dying and resurrecting from death to life, he is able to set us free. He gives us life by his death.

Our freedom is his joy.

Wright further explains, "As go'el, therefore, God will exert himself to whatever extent is necessary on their behalf for their [Israel's] protection or rescue." This is the mission of God: to extend his reach into all the Earth, to protect, and to be father and family champion for all people. It's why he is the rescuer, the redeemer, and the hope for the world.

And he doesn't stop there. The radical thing about God's plan to redeem is that he invites the redeemed to partner with him in spreading the redemption and healing around like passing out party invitations.

Jesus empowers those who know his healing to extend it to others. John 13:34–35 exhorts the sons and daughters of God to "love one another. As I have loved you, so you must love one another. By this everyone will know that you are my disciples, if you love one another."

I saw this type of life-transforming healing take place at the motel time and time again. All because someone was willing to allow for an interruption in their day—willing to sit and listen to someone in a motel room share their story. Healing happened as people were seen and known and cared for. Visiting the motel often felt like an interruption in my day, but I left with a renewed hope and excitement for the healing and restoration Jesus was delivering to those he saw and loved.

Spending time with his people is never an interruption for Jesus. He does not have more important things to do or more important people to be with today. For me and you, he has all the time in the world.

God doesn't expect you or me to be the *go'el redeemer* who takes care of all the daunting global issues we face today. Rest easy, that's his job. He only asks that we serve those around us, those in our spheres of influence, out of love, in the same manner he has loved us. The healed can extend healing to others by allowing for their interruptions and stopping, turning towards them, and listening to them with compassion and care. When this happens, healing happens.

No one is outside the scope of the healing Jesus is able and willing to give.

In a world questioning the goodness and presence of God, we can get off the sidelines, go to him with our need, receive his healing, and be part of his healing of those around us. It could be as simple as buying a coffee for the most awkward person in the office. Or putting the teakettle on for the widow on your block.

To be seen and known is to bring about healing.

That's for sure.

PART TWO

Grow Alongside Him

Every morning before my son leaves for school, I pack him a sack lunch for the day. I don't bother to pack tomorrow's lunch or the next day's, because they wouldn't be fresh tomorrow or the next day. And I'm not exactly sure what all goes down on the school campus, but most days, his backpack comes home looking like it's been to war. I have a sneaking suspicion tomorrow's lunch would be a casualty if it went with him early.

In the same way, Jesus gives us exactly what we need to sustain us today. He has tomorrow worked out. We need only to keep our attention on him today. Easier said than done, I know.

CARRIE ELLEN

My four-year-old reminds me how difficult it is to live in the today. At his age, he's learning what yesterday, today, and tomorrow mean. "But yesterday you said it was today, so how can today be today, when you said it was today yesterday?" He gets even more confused about tomorrow because tomorrow is always tomorrow and never quite seems to come. Who's on first, anybody?

As their mom, I want both of my boys to enjoy the day. I don't want them dwelling on yesterday or tomorrow. That type of focus and thinking leads straight to Regret Boulevard and Anxiety Lane. I simply want them to live in the today and do their thing in the moment they are in. Isn't that the truth for all of us?

We were designed to live in the moment. To be present. To rest in God's provision and care of us for all things and to walk in step with him throughout our everyday moments and experiences, be it folding laundry or going on safari.

To the wilderness-wandering Israelites, God gave only enough food—manna—for one day at a time. The twelve disciples of Jesus were sent out empty-handed so that they might be cared for one day at a time. Jesus longs to be the only reserve we need. He wants our full attention today because he knows he's the only one who can give us what we need to sustain us in this crazy life, one day at a time.

We aren't built to carry more than that and why would we want to?

Jesus had several mic-drop moments when he walked the earth and Matthew 6:34 is one of them: "Therefore do not worry about tomorrow, for tomorrow will worry about itself. Each day has enough trouble of its own."

As a mom, I want my boys to enjoy their child-hood and the moment they are in right now. My nine-year-old cannot wait to be a teen and my four-year-old cannot wait to be five—then six, then seven, and so on. I tell them all the time, "Slow your roll, kids."

Let's slow our roll, friends. Let's resolve to slow down enough to catch our breath. Let's walk, not run, the next mile and do our best to be present. In a crazy mysterious way, Jesus shows up with compassion in the now. His presence with us today heals our past and provides for our future. We need only to rest and trust him for today.

While there are many gifts Jesus freely gives us in order to sustain us, in the next four chapters we're going to highlight four particular gifts that I hope will help us rest today. We will focus our time on the gift of his presence and availability to us at all times. We'll see that his gift of healing is available today. We'll discover friendship with Jesus is not only possible, it's a gift our souls desperately need. And finally, we'll see that he freely offers us the gift of partnering with him to bring heaven to earth.

So, grab your sack lunch and let's move out. God's got goodness awaiting us today.

CHAPTER 5

Crash

We were teens on a joyride. I was at the wheel. My friend Candace was in the passenger side of my ride. Two of my cousins and one of their friends were squeezed into the back seat of my white, four-door 1997 Nissan Sentra. My friend Melinda said it looked like a marshmallow. She was right.

In our collective teenage minds, we decided it would be a good idea to drive the roller coaster–like streets of Laguna Hills in southern California. I may have been a little overconfident in my driving abilities as a new license holder. We took the hills with the windows down and nineties tunes blasting through the speakers. All was fun and games until we started down a steep hill a little too fast and I misjudged how much braking was needed to slow the marshmallow down enough to make a left at the bottom of the hill.

I missed the turn and crashed head-on into a guardrail. Thankfully, no one was hurt but the marshmallow.

Crash.

I am happy to report that my driving skills have improved over the years and I haven't crashed a car since. I am, however, on the receiving end of numerous crash collisions caused by my J Men.

The J Men are no strangers to bangs and bruises. They play hard. They run fast. They crash into each other and their surroundings like it's their job. As their mom, I am typically on the receiving end of their pileups. And because they are still young, we're in this sweet season when they run to me for all things. I have the constant bruises to prove their impacts on my middle-aged person.

They are still little and confident in my love for them. Which is to say, they don't hesitate to run straight into my arms when they need me or have something exciting to share. They have no issue running to me anytime, anyplace, about anything.

I know this innocent trust of me won't last forever. And, really, it shouldn't. It would be weird for them to charge at me when they're adults and I'm an old lady. That might land them a night in county jail. But for now, while they still choose to come to me with hurts and pain, giggles, silly stories, and more, I will gladly wear the bruises that come with their collisions into me like a winter coat.

If I love it when my boys run to me in their need and joy, how much more does God, our loving Father, love it when we run to him with our need and joy?

In the last chapter, we glanced quickly at the story of the bleeding woman who crashed into Jesus and it changed her life forever. Her bleeding stopped *and* her soul was restored to its rightful place as a daughter in the family of God.

Most of us probably don't have a chronic bleeding disorder. But all of us live with some form of brokenness and hardship. We all have struggles, pain, trauma, disappointment, and so on for which we desperately need healing. I think sometimes it's easier to believe healing is possible when it's someone else who needs it. But when it comes to areas of pain and brokenness in our life, well, we just aren't sure if healing is for us too.

For years I put off crashing into Jesus with my own need and brokenness because I was afraid of being exposed and of what that might mean for me and for those around me. I was afraid I'd be the one who would stop Jesus in his tracks. If I came clean to him about my pain and trauma, I'd be the one who would stump him and he just wouldn't be able to help me. And if he could, he wouldn't heal me today; no, healing would come after I died and went to heaven, where every sin and shameful act is finally forgotten for eternity.

But those thoughts were a lie and an assault on Jesus' abilities and desires for those he created out of his unwavering love. He's not afraid of anything you may be experiencing or facing today. He has authority over everything in your life in this moment. He is actively working to heal and restore the places in your life where you are in need. And not only for a future day and time; rather, Jesus is ready and able to heal right now. And while the timing of healing and restoration may not unfold in the way we expect, I firmly believe Jesus is busy working to bring the specific healing we need right now.

We are free to crash into him today.

This reminds me of a time some kids were brought to Jesus for a blessing. The disciples got irritated by the kids and tried to make them go away. When I was a kid in Sunday school, this scene was illustrated with flannelgraphs. Flannel

Jesus had well-conditioned, thick Fabio hair, and a blue sash draped perfectly over his shoulder. His smile was gentle and his teeth appeared freshly bleached. The flannelgraph children looked well-groomed and lined up on the flannelgraph board in single file before Jesus. They patiently waited to receive their blessing and a pat on the tops of their heads—with neatly combed hair, of course.

Now that I'm a mom, the eighties are over and flannelgraphs are vintage, that scene is comical. A realistic illustration of the scene might look more like my description of my kids running and crashing into me. Kids do not walk anywhere. They run everywhere. I'm willing to bet my daily four cups of piping-hot black coffee that the kids in this Bible story ran and crashed into Jesus, causing him to lose his balance and hop on one foot to avoid falling to the ground.

I imagine they had gnarly bed head and feet coated in a mixture of mud and goat poop. Their breath was likely more deadly than the fiercest of armies. Their fingers were sticky from unidentifiable gobbledygook and their chatter and giggles as loud as a high school marching band.

Back in Bible days, kids were often viewed as a nuisance. They were expected to remain unseen and out of the way of adults, especially the men. As the story unfolds, the disciples, clearly annoyed by the invasion of children before Jesus, rebuked them. But Jesus wasn't at all annoyed as the kids ran towards him. Jesus is never annoyed when his people go to him. Indeed, the Bible tells us he was none too pleased with the disciples' attempts to prevent the kids from his presence.

"'Let the little children come to me, and do not hinder them, for the kingdom of God belongs to such as these. Truly I tell you, anyone who will not receive the kingdom of God like a little child will never enter it.' And he took the children in his arms, placed his hands on them and blessed them."[1]

Jesus loves it when we approach him like children. In other words, when we approach him just as we are.

He is glad that we crash into him when:

We're a hot mess.

We left the house and forgot to put shoes on.

We're excited about something happening in our lives.

We're disappointed about something happening in our lives.

We're in pain and struggling.

We're drowning in the mundane.

We're confused.

We doubt.

We're angry at our sister or brother.

We want to strangle our spouse.

We feel insecure at work or school.

We're worried about our kids.

We're sick. We're tired. We are so over all the things.

No matter what's on our minds and swirling around in our hearts, Jesus longs for all of us to take it all to him. To crash into him with who we are and what we are experiencing today.

We were made to live in such close proximity to Jesus that we feel free enough to run into his arms and throw him off balance anytime, anywhere, for any reason.

———————

To school the adults with what the kids already knew about crashing into Jesus, he gave them—and us—another example of an incredible and life-changing crash story in the Gospels.

Jesus, illustrating what his kingdom is like, told the story of the youngest son of an affluent man who asked for his inheritance early, only to leave his father's house, travel to a distant country, and squander the fortune.

In trying to gain it all, the youngest son lost it all. Away from home and his family, the son exchanged dependence upon his father for independence from him, and it cost him everything.

When the son lost not only all he had, but who he was, he hit rock bottom and decided to go home. On his journey home, full of shame, he conjured up an apology he'd give to his dad, in hopes he would be allowed to return home, even if it meant he'd work like a slave for his dad from then on.

But before the son could get a word out, look what the father did: "But while he was still a long way off, his father saw him and was filled with compassion for him; he ran to his son, threw his arms around him and kissed him" (Luke 15:20).

Crash.

The dad didn't just miss his son and mope in his La-Z-Boy recliner every evening. Jesus tells us that the father saw the son when he was still far off, implying the father stood watch, eager and hopeful that his son would return home. We get the picture that at the first sight of his lost son walking towards home, the dad, a man of honor, who culturally would've worn a fancy robe, likely dishonored himself by pulling up his robe to run towards the son. He tightly embraced him, which I'd like to imagine was more of a tackle-to-the-ground-best-bear-hug-ever. The son never got all the words of his apology speech out. The father literally wrapped himself around the son, covering him, embracing him, welcoming him home. And finally, he had a robe of honor placed around his son, who was now home, where he belonged.

Jesus told the story as an illustration of what God is like. God is so eager to have you and me and all those around us home, the place of ganan we talked about in chapter three. He will never stop pursuing us. He will never stop keeping watch for us. Even when you are "a long way off," you're never too far off from him. He is always nearby. He's like the nosey neighbor who peeks out the curtains to see who's barreling down the street. He will never stop keeping watch for you. He is full of mercy and grace.

And his mercy and grace have no problem colliding with your pain. In fact, it's the very nature of God's mercy and grace to put themselves on a collision course with your hurt and pain. When you take your sadness, brokenness, and pain to him, a wild, supernatural exchange takes place. Jesus can, and longs to, take on your pain—even to the point of wearing it like a sweater—and, in its place, to clothe you with peace and joy.

Isaiah 53:5 illuminates the beauty of the nature of Christ in this way: "But he was pierced for our transgressions, he was crushed for our iniquities; the punishment that brought us peace was upon him, and by his wounds we are healed."

Jesus grabbed hold of sin and squelched the power it once held in order to replace the strife and pain sin caused with peace, protection, and healing.

Crash.

When my boys crash into me with their hurt, it's worth every bruise. If I willingly exchange my comfort for theirs in their time of need, how much more does Jesus willingly take on the pain you carry? You were made to crash into him with all you've got. Giving up your felt pain to him today will result in you being wrapped in a blanket of peace and healing.

I witnessed a pain-for-peace exchange firsthand

in the Democratic Republic of Congo (DRC). The House of Peace, an orphanage and hospice operated by Catholic nuns, lives in a state of constant crash collisions of pain and peace.

The group I was with entered through large iron gates that opened into a quad area, with a building to our left and another to our right. Several children played in the quad. I remember a boy who was about nine. He wore ragged pink overalls and had a bad case of the giggles. He didn't speak a word, but joy oozed out of him. A small playground set sat adjacent to the quad, and there more children squealed as they sat on the swings and flung their little bodies down the slide.

After playing with the children in the quad for a bit, we entered the building on the left. On the inside, we found more nuns caring for a handful of babies. One little guy grabbed my attention with his piercing stare and crooked smile. Through a translator, we learned he had been found in a plastic bag on the side of the road. A snake was also found in the bag. Miraculously, the baby was unharmed by the snake. The nuns named him Moses.

The inspirational and kind nuns had created a refuge for the playful, giggly children. There was life and hope at the orphanage located on the left of the quad. When it was time to cross the quad and enter the building on the right, I wasn't prepared for what I saw.

Above the entrance hung a sign that said "House of Peace." The building had two large rooms connected by a hallway. The breeze blew through large open windows. I was thankful for the fresh air. We walked through the first great room where, lying on paper-thin mattresses, were a handful of men and women suffering from HIV/AIDS.

One man struggled to lift his head just enough to say, "Remember us when you return to America." He had no idea that he was impossible to forget. In the hallway that connected the two great rooms, a dying woman lay lifeless. I stood next to her side for a few minutes and held her cold, skin-and-bones hand. She was too weak to open her eyes or make any movement. The only sign of life was her shallow breath in and out.

In the second large room were a few more patients, alive by the thinnest thread. One lay on the hard concrete floor to stay cool. I stood in the middle of the room, completely overwhelmed with the need that surrounded me. I felt a tidal wave of helplessness rush over me and it was all I could do to simply stand.

My friend Tami stood next to me. We were encouraged to pray. I couldn't. I simply stood there, overcome with emotion and the felt need for something far greater than my words could deliver.

An intersection of life and death exists at the House of Peace. In that moment, I felt the weighty reality of just how thin the line is between life and death. I was paralyzed by the juxtaposition of the life I witnessed on the left side of the quad and the hopeless right side that reeked of death and sadness.

The nuns at the House of Peace tended to the sick. They did their best to comfort the dying and to ease their pain. They stood by the side of the hurting and, in this way, brought comfort and care.

Whether in Congo or Illinois, isn't this what we collectively long for in the midst of our pain? The comfort and assurance to know we are not alone? To know peace in the midst of our pain? We can't escape suffering in this world, be it from an illness, divorce, disappointment, or abuse. Yet, as the House of Peace bears witness to, suffering isn't the end of the story.

Pain and hope can coexist.

This example doesn't scratch the surface of the reality of pain and suffering the world experiences daily. I know it doesn't even begin to understand the pain and hurt you know to be true in your life. Your hurt is no less a concern to Jesus than the pain of those at the House of Peace. He sees your pain.

He lived the human experience so that he could collide with your pain, take your pain, heal your pain.

Jesus doesn't just invite us to approach him when we are well-behaved, cleaned up, hair washed and brushed, teeth white, and looking all put together with our Sunday best on. Our lives are not 1980s flannelgraphs. We are invited to crash into Jesus while aboard our own personal hot-mess express. Jesus' invitation to a collision with him is simple: "Come to me, all you who are weary and burdened, and I will give you rest."[2]

Jesus invites you and me to crash into and collide with him; to bring the mess, the struggle, the chaos, and the poverty of our hearts; to come exposed and believing he will receive us in a loving embrace. He'll take the hit and not mind the bruising from the impact in the least. In fact, it brings him joy to take our pain and replace it with peace.[3]

Only a collision with Jesus will set us on a path towards hope and healing.

Psalm 116:2 says God bends his ear towards us. He wants to hear from us. He's a loving father bracing himself for impact, ready and waiting for you and me to crash into him.

He wants nothing more than to be by our sides in and through every circumstance of our lives.

The world tells us to run to all the things *but* Jesus. It lures us to collide with Netflix and binge-watch movies and TV shows, drink too much, or zone out scrolling social media. But these are lies and will only deepen the well of our pain.

Jesus is a better way.

Run to Jesus like a child. Crash into him and trust that he'll receive you in the biggest and best bear hug you could imagine. He is filled with compassion for you. He will meet you aboard your hot-mess express with open arms to welcome you home.

That's for sure.

CHAPTER 6

Drop Your Jar and Run

There was no denying it: the Romanian monk was drunk.

Monk man and I stood in the middle of the large monastery where he lived and worked. He asked me to take his picture. He stood tall and proud, with a smile on his face and hands behind his back. Behind him was a water well, where just moments before he had carefully showed me how to draw the water up using a wooden bucket and a rope pulley. He was blitzed, and excited to teach me how to draw up water from the well.

I wondered if there was a little something more than just water in that well, if you're picking up what I'm putting down.

There are several prominent stories involving wells in the Bible. Jesus' friend John wrote about one of them in his namesake Gospel.[1]

We don't get her name, but we read about a woman who was ostracized by her community and, likely, largely misunderstood. As a result, she chose to draw water from the well later in the day so she could avoid the stares, nasty comments, and annoying eye rolls of the other women in the town.

Those around the woman might have thought they knew her because of her actions, but Jesus knew who she was deep down, in the well of her soul.

As the story unfolds in John's gospel account, we find her hidden behind her water jar and skeptical of Jesus. And who could blame her? She had been married many times and was likely riddled with shame and guilt. Today, we're often taught she felt shame because her multiple husbands were simply proof that she was the town hussy. But considering the culture and time in which she lived, I can't help but speculate there may have been more to the story. For example, in her culture, if she struggled with infertility, that was cause for divorce. Having a child to pass down an inheritance to was a big deal during that time period and within that culture.

Regardless of what one might speculate about the woman behind the jar at the well, Jesus knew exactly who she was and what was hidden deep in the well of her heart. Jesus saw her trauma, abuse, and shame, and he saw through it and beyond it into who she was. His desire was for her to hide in him, not from him.

When Jesus looked at her from across the well of water, he saw directly into the well of her created soul, seeing the woman he had made. He saw his daughter, crafted and formed by his very hands. He saw a woman created to bear his image. He saw the woman he had fashioned for a purpose. Her very breath spoke of his name.

The moment she realized Jesus was indeed the Messiah, she dropped the water jug, the very thing she hid behind. She slipped on her kicks and ran back to the very people she used to hide from. And she told them of the man "who told me everything I ever did." The thing she worked so hard to keep hidden was now the very thing she led with as she proclaimed that the long-awaited Messiah was on the scene.

Her story was not about what she had or had not done. Her story was about what Jesus had done. And this changed everything.

Long ago, Jesus thought of and designed the woman at the well. He allowed the struggles she faced and then he showed up with compassion to turn her struggles into shouts that declared who he was to an entire town that ultimately put their trust in Jesus. Nothing is wasted with Jesus.

Girlfriend at the well is a story of the hurt and pain we all know in the same way we know tacos belong to Tuesday. Jesus took her pain and then drew up out of her the person he'd made her to be, the one who would preach the good news to her people.

———————————

For years, I hid behind a "jar" of shame and suppressed the God-given gifts he designed me with out of fear of being exposed. What if people really knew how selfish I was? What if they caught sight of my anger? What if others knew about my trauma and the things I had done? Even *I* don't want to see the struggles lying at the bottom of the well of my soul.

Part of living in the moment and in the fullness of who he made us to be is recognizing our daily need for an encounter with Jesus. Daily, Jesus invites us to meet with him so that he can remind us who we are and what we are purposed for. We have to be willing to drop the "jar" and allow him to draw his design for us up out of us.

My drop-the-jar-and-run moment came in 2018 when I was seven or eight months pregnant with my youngest J Man. Throughout that year, some trauma from my past had welled up and I couldn't shake it. Part of it may have been because I was approaching forty (how did that happen?) and I couldn't stand the thought of entering another decade still holding on to pain and hurts from years past. Can I get a witness? Another part of it was the baby I was carrying. As a mom of one son already, soon to become a boy mom of two, I so desired to be a healthy and healed mom for my kids.

I had been carrying around pain for a long time and not because I didn't believe Jesus could and would heal me and free me of it, but because I simply was more comfortable keeping it lodged deep down than I was talking to him or anyone else about it. For years I chose to keep my pain quiet and hidden within me for fear of exposing myself too much and because it was just too hard. I didn't want to deal with it. I'd been lugging the weight of the jar around this long; what's another five, ten, twenty years?

And because Jesus is too kind to leave you and me in a world of pain, I believe he was behind the welling up of the past, and I believe he allowed it so that he could set me free from the shame and pain and all the things that come from shoving hurt deep down into the well of our souls.

Jesus longs to heal the hurt.

I called up a trusted friend and asked her to meet me for coffee. Kaycee's laughter is infectious. Coming straight from her gut, her deep belly laugh makes you feel as if you're the funniest person in her world. When you speak, she leans in to listen, catching every word. She's down for a good story or a funny joke any time of day. She's present. She's engaging. She's a true friend.

Kaycee and I first met when we showed up at a stranger's house, along with about ten other women, for a Bible study.

Now listen, the extrovert in me is all for meeting new people. Yet going to a stranger's house is about the scariest thing you can ask me to do and for one reason only.

Cats.

Is the homeowner a cat person? Are house cats

lurking around, hiding out, waiting and ready to pounce on me as I enter their home?

Cats are vile creatures and cannot be trusted.

The first night of the study, my anxiety level over whether I would encounter a cat at a stranger's house, along with how I would respond around a group of ladies I was meeting for the first time amongst said cats, was at an all-time high. As in, it was back-of-the-neck-tingling, hair-raising anxiety.

On that first night, I was so relieved to not square off with a creepy feline, and also to have met Kaycee. I knew that night I wanted to be her friend.

Several weeks of the study went by and you'll be happy to hear there were no cat sightings and my friendship with Kaycee only grew.

On one particular night of the study, we created space for each person to share a lie they believed to be true about themselves and then to counter that lie with the truth of what Jesus says. The idea was to tear down the lie and build up the truth. We took turns sharing.

Moving clockwise around the room, Kaycee was at two o'clock. I was at four. She was brave and shared without inhibition. She just laid it all out. I knew she was cool before this moment, but she blew my mind with her honesty, vulnerability, and maturity as she shared her struggles. Like her glorious laugh, her authenticity was contagious. I resonated with what she shared. I had believed the same lie and it had manifested itself into my life in very similar ways. But I wasn't as brave as Kaycee that night.

When it was my turn to share, I did share a lie and I countered it with the truth of Jesus, of course, but I wasn't about to get real-real like Kaycee did.

We can't force healing. Healing is Jesus' jam, and he does it in his timing and in his perfect way.

While I didn't open up about our shared experiences that night, Kaycee's real talk paved the way for me to eventually get there. Six years after that night of sharing, we sat on the patio of a café on a cool Southern California evening. Sipping from our giant latte mugs, Kaycee listened and I spewed all the things. I shared with her things that had happened to me as a child, that had resulted in me believing lies, that led to my own behavior that only furthered the lies and hurt. In essence, I laid it all out much like she had six years earlier.

When I was done and had sipped the last of my latte, Kaycee sat across from me and smiled. There was no condemnation nor condoning. She simply listened and, to my surprise, she exercised phenomenal control of her face and its many potential expressions. I could learn a thing or two about controlling my face from her. She was neither shocked nor taken aback.

Kaycee didn't offer any solutions or make any excuses. She didn't even curse the offenders in my life. She listened, she heard me, she saw me, and she graciously reminded me of who I was. Who I truly was, made by the maker of all things good and lovely—the one who, because he is good and lovely, made me good and lovely too. She reminded me that I was fashioned and handmade by the Creator himself. She didn't quote Bible verses at me or hurl cheesy words my way, as so often people do when they don't know what to say.

She simply pointed me to the cross and to the forgiveness that I already knew to be true.

That conversation was the beginning of me loosening my grip on the water jar that had masked the reality of who Jesus was and what he had to say about me. I'm not the strongest lady in the gym and my arms were shaky as I attempted to hold the jar up in front of me everywhere I went and in every conversation I had. I was weary from holding that water jar. It needed to fall. It needed to break because of all the lies and garbage it represented.

When the jar drops and shatters into tiny shards, it loses its power, and in its place, freedom and a life of flourishing as God designed begin.

I tell you this story because life is short. There is no need to wait for anything or anyone before running to Jesus and unveiling your struggles and your pain to him. He will exchange your struggles for security in who he created you to be. He will take your hurt and, in its place, give you the healing you need. He will hold your pain and will turn it into your purpose. He will take your regrets and, in their place, give you rest.

That group of women who started out as strangers getting together to talk about Jesus continued to meet for about two years. We became close enough for them to know I was not a fan of the feline. It must have been several months into our time together when my worst nightmare happened.

As I sat in my usual chair, something furry and frightening waltzed by in my peripheral vision. Yes, you guessed it. A cat! Not just any cat. The biggest, furriest cat in the history of the world. I sat still in a quiet panic, my stiff neck slowly turning my face directly towards the furry beast.

The eyes around the room looked from me and then to the cat. While I sat frozen in fear, the room erupted into laughter, followed by the shock and scurry of the homeowner who had no idea her cat had escaped her room and was on the prowl, looking for its next victim (me!) throughout the house. She removed the cat from the room and I was finally able to exhale the breath I had been holding, nearly cutting off oxygen to my brain. Tragedy averted.

Here's the thing. My disdain for vile cats was and is so legit, had I seen that cat on night one of that group meeting together, I would not have returned. I would have allowed my fear of felines to keep me from experiencing the friendship that led to my healing.

What fears are holding you back from experiencing life lived to the fullest? Fear is a trap that just loves to remind us of our failures. My fear of cats and of calling out the lies in my life could have led me to loneliness and isolation and a life hidden from Christ. I don't want that for my life, and I certainly don't want it for yours.

Jesus knows our thoughts, our desires, our struggles, the weight we carry today, and the depths of our souls. He looks upon us with unlimited mercy, grace, and love. The patient, kind, loving care Jesus extended to the woman at the well is available to us too.

Identify and name your fears and the lies you've believed and then find your person, someone who you trust and who will no doubt speak truth and love over you as if Jesus himself were seated across from you, sipping on a latte and smiling at you with kindness in his eyes. After all, kindness is what he's about and who he is. It flows out of him like breath in and out of his lungs. He is a well of kindness, mercy, and grace that never runs dry. Maybe that's why he said those who drink from his well of living waters will never thirst again.

Freedom is found in the emptying of our failings and brokenness.

The drunk monk cast down a wooden bucket only to draw up water. Jesus desires to draw up and out of us the truth and goodness of who he made us to be. He wants to fill us with purpose and peace.

Drop the jar.
Thirst no more.
That's for sure.

CHAPTER 7

Couch Coffee Chats

When my family relocated from the blessed Golden State of California to the Lone Star State of Texas recently, I was reminded of something my friend Jamie once said to me when I moved to Massachusetts for grad school twenty years ago. Jamie advised me to fill my time in my new state with Jesus. "Talk to him. Fill his ears up with what's on your heart and mind," she said.

I was facing the absence of friends and familiarity, and she was encouraging me to create time apart with Jesus to fill those now-empty spaces.

The truth that Jesus wants to be both Lord and friend to you and me is one of the greatest mysteries and miracles of Jesus. On one hand, he is the all-knowing and all-powerful God who spoke the created world into existence. *And* he is closer than a brother and calls us friends. Jesus came to serve, to rescue, to restore, and to be our life's trail guide, leading us back home to the presence of God the Father. And along the way, he constantly reminds us and shapes us more and more into who he made us to be.

He is not a God who orchestrates life's events from afar, rather, he's knee-deep in all our circumstances today. He's in the trenches with us. He willingly comes alongside you and me in the mundane of our daily lives as a friend. His friendship is one of the greatest gifts given to us to help us navigate life.

Friends.[1] I probably don't need to say more than that and you already know exactly what I'm referring to. Chances are, you've seen every episode dozens of times. You're likely thinking of your favorite episode or line as you read this. *Friends* revolutionized the world of television when it debuted in 1994. Before *Friends* was available, shows that portrayed American families, like *Full House*, *The Cosby Show*, *Family Matters*, and several others, dominated TV. *Friends* broke out of the family mold and into a new space: the world of a group of single friends living in NYC. The series was an incredible hit that continues to be watched and loved by many even now, close to thirty years later.

I can't help but wonder if *Friends* was and continues to be such a hit because it tapped into one of humanity's most basic needs: the need for friendship.

If we're honest, we crave the kind of friendship the *Friends* theme song suggests. We long for the confidence and assurance that others will be there for us when we need them most.

Having a trusted friend who we know will stick with us, regardless of our circumstances, and who will not run away, no matter what type of crazy may come flying out our mouths at times, is more valuable than a heaping pile of gold bricks.

To have deep, meaningful friendships with those who get us is a universal desire. We need this kind of friendship: the kind that accepts, builds up, exercises patience, and demonstrates purpose. There's something in our build that desires trusting and supportive friendship and I'm convinced this longing stems from the way things were when God first created Adam and Eve.

In his timely book for our generation, *Your Longing Has a Name*,[2] author Dominic Done draws attention to the one thing in the creation story God says isn't good. We spent a lot of time in the first part of this book focusing on the goodness

God created in the world and in Adam and Eve. However, as Done points out, there is one thing God says isn't good in the creation story, and that's for man to be alone.

This is countercultural for us today. The message our culture mass-produces is vastly different from God's design. We are pressured to believe that nobody can be trusted—that we are all we need to accomplish what's best for us. The very thing God said was not good, to be alone, is the very thing our individualistic culture claims is all we need.

It's hogwash, people. We need authentic, genuine, caring friendship with each other and with Jesus.

God created us for friendship. He designed and purposed us for vibrant and trusting friendship with one another. He knows this world is tough, and Netflix and a gallon of ice cream just won't cut it to carry us through all the confusion, difficulties, disappointments, and pain we face in this life. We are wired for companionship and for friendships of mutual support and trust. Without friendship, we become isolated and, as God said long ago, "It is not good."[3]

———————

When I was a teenager, I was part of a youth group at our little country Baptist church. We met for Sunday school on Sunday mornings, spent a lot of Sunday afternoons in the fellowship hall eating church lady casseroles (ick) and playing wiffle ball in the quad. As if that wasn't enough time together, after a short trip home to change into more casual church clothes and guzzle down a cold glass of nineties Tang (double ick), we'd return on Sunday nights for a less formal church service. On Wednesday nights, we'd gather again around a bonfire in a backyard for youth group.

It's roughly three decades later and I remain friends with four girls from this youth group. We have a group text thread that blows up my phone on the daily. We went to different high schools and lived in different parts of town, but attending youth group together was where we connected and grew our friendship. We had no idea then, when we sat in church together and passed notes and as we sat around the bonfire inhaling way too much fire smoke, how much we would need each other as adults.

We've been there for each other through infertility, miscarriages, and challenging pregnancies. We've celebrated the eleven kids among the five of us, five of whom were born in an eight-month span. We've been each other's sounding boards when thinking through many of life's difficult decisions. We've carried each other through seasons of grief and loss. We talk about Jesus and the ridiculousness found on TikTok in the same breath. We make each other laugh until it hurts and our faces leak in all possible ways. We once sailed out of the harbor and into the seas of Newport Beach, California, chasing dolphins while we dined on overpriced avocado toast, because, well, we fancy like that. We have endured and celebrated decades of life together.

Shared experiences are often the Gorilla Glue that bond friendships together for the long haul. And I've come to believe it's in shared experiences with Jesus that we form friendship with him.

Jesus gets the human experience of longing for authentic relationship better than any of us. He died alone so that we might never be alone. He was isolated on the cross so that we might never face isolation.

The moment the resurrection took place and God raised him from the dead, Jesus made possible the restoration of our relationship with God first, followed by the restoration of our relationships with those around us. He shared in our human experience in order to rescue us from all we go through in our lives. And he does so in the most intimate and personal ways, as a friend.

For many years, I heard people refer to Jesus as their friend. But it wasn't until I experienced a season of disappointment—something he knew well in his humanity—that I came to know his friendship personally.

I've come to believe Jesus allows us to experience disappointments and the pesky unwanted loneliness that seem to follow disappointment around like a puppy dog so that he can give us life-giving friendship with him. He experienced disappointment and loneliness to the fullest as he hung on a cross and took his final breath.

If you are aboard the Enneagram train, you'll

know what I mean when I confess that I am an Enneagram seven. If you're like, Enneagram what? Don't sweat it. It's a personality test to help you understand yourself and the whys behind your behavior and the decisions you make. It's also helpful in better understanding the people around you.

As an Enneagram seven, I am all about the fun. I love experiencing new things. I live for adventure and love being in the state of "what's next?" Pre-mamahood, it was not out of the ordinary for me to call up a friend and suggest we fly to San Francisco for the day or take a spontaneous road trip across state lines. I cruise around town with sports equipment, beach towels, and extra clothes in the car because you never know when adventure may strike.

One spring during my years in Massachusetts, it literally rained for two weeks straight. This California girl was going to shrivel up and die if sunshine was not found fast. I called up a friend from school, Searan, and asked her to go with me in search of sunshine. Thankfully, Searan agreed and we hit the road, headed south and west. Destination? Wherever the glorious sun was found shining upon the people.

After twenty-one hours of driving, and a lot of Tupac and Young MC bumping through the speakers of my beloved 1998 black 4Runner, we found the sun warmly shining upon the people of Nashville. We met up with our friend Genevieve, who was from Nashville, crashed at her parents' home, and soaked up as many sunrays as possible before driving back up to gloomy New England after a few days.

Because Enneagram seven people are here for the party, we tend to be painfully awkward when it comes to all things sad. I am the girl who laughs at the worst time to laugh because it's my way of coping with how uncomfortable pain and sadness make me feel. It can be very annoying for people around me who are more comfortable than I am with sitting in sadness and grief awhile.

When I'm uncomfortable, I fight the urge to crack jokes to cut the tension in a room of sadness. Even in the most difficult of circumstances, I see the silver lining, the hope of what could be on the other side of tragedy and bad news. I'm the glass-is-always-full girl. No, scratch that—not just half full, but overflowing. Let's shove the sad stuff down and move on to the sunshine and rainbows as quickly as possible, please.

Hence my reaction to the said disappointment in my life. I was told my job—a job I absolutely loved and felt tremendous purpose in—had been eliminated. And I laughed. Not exactly the reaction my boss expected in that moment.

Disappointment is such a Debbie Downer. Almost immediately upon losing my job, I felt the tug-of-war pull to disengage and withdraw from those around me as a result of my felt disappointment. Disappointment is like a thief who desires to rob us of all purpose and joy. Feelings of disappointment tend to lead us down a path of isolation.

On the flip side, because of Jesus' shared experience of disappointment, and because it's his business to make sad things come untrue, he can take our disappointment and turn it into an invitation for friendship with him.

He longs to be our friend. Whether it's disappointment like I experienced, or it's depression, disease, divorce, discouragement, desperation, and so on, Jesus has purposed us to take it all to him. He's the friend who can be trusted and who will always be there for us.

While just the thought of disappointment is enough to give me heart palpitations, I've learned through experience to not be afraid of it anymore. Disappointment and its companion, loneliness, are an invitation extended to us by Jesus that leads us to friendship with him.

Jonathan Evans says, "Your greatest ministry comes out of your greatest misery."[4]

I didn't set out to become friends with Jesus. He simply showed up when I needed him. He was available and kind. Over time, and after a lot of difficult early morning coffee chats with him on my couch about my disappointments, I began to see and know he was in my circumstances with me. This is friendship. He became my friend through many early morning couch coffee chats.

God specifically designed you and me to be his friends—to engage with him about all things all day—and then to extend that type of friendship to those around us. If Jesus were here in the flesh today, he'd be the guy blowing up your phone with memes and random jokes to make you laugh while you're in that dreaded meeting with your boss. And he'd be the guy to show up on your doorstep after your long day, with a tub of pistachio ice cream, to sit with you, listen to you with compassion, and encourage you with the truth of who he is and who he made you to be.

When I walked through my season of disappointment, Jesus showed up on my couch for early morning coffee chats. Over time, as I sipped my Trader Joe's French roast black coffee and unloaded my mind and my heart to him, he became my friend. He sat with me in the stillness on my couch in those early dawn hours.

Sometimes Jesus will allow us to walk through and experience the hard stuff in order to get to the good stuff he has designed for us.

He will allow seasons of heavy burdens, so that we look to him to find relief. He knows that when we keep our eyes fixed on him, he can and will take the weight off our shoulders and replace it with his peace.

He's given us many examples of friendships in the Bible. Mary had Elizabeth, who shared in the experience of a first and very unexpectant pregnancy with her. David and Jonathan had each other as they navigated life under the scary rule of Jonathan's dad, King Saul. Brothers Moses and

Aaron were buddied up to lead one of the greatest rescues from slavery in history. Paul and Timothy took the church across borders, ethnicities, and generations together. Elijah and Elisha were friends who heard from God and shared his words of life and freedom with the people of their day.

We were not meant to live our lives alone. One of Jesus' greatest gifts to us is friendship. He knows exactly what we need to survive our day and he's created the buddy system to help us walk out life's ups and downs together.

Speaking of David, David knew a thing or two about the Lord carrying the load on his back. The book of Psalms is full of David's conversations— cave chats if you will—with God about David's disappointments and struggles, such as when he ran for his life from Saul. As a result of these events, he knew things to be true about God that he could have only been certain of because of his troubles that drove him to God for help. He said things like, "Cast your cares on the LORD and he will sustain you; he will never let the righteous be shaken."[5]

You only get to know for certain that God will sustain you when you've been on the verge of losing it all.

David's words are meant to encourage us to let Jesus carry the loads we have strapped to our backs. Let Jesus be the friend you get real with. Drop the f-bomb if you need to. He can handle it. You cannot shock him or shake him.

Give him the backpack burden weighing your shoulders down. Nothing about you or your life is too heavy for him. He already endured the cross for you. There is absolutely nothing new to him nor anything you may or may not do that will change the immense love he poured out for you upon the cross.

When my sons were little with little legs, they were limited in how far they could walk before their legs would quit on them. That didn't stop me and my husband from taking them on long hikes we knew they couldn't walk on their own. We knew before we arrived at the trailhead that we'd need to carry them at some point along the way, but this didn't discourage us from going; we went anyway.

Neither of us minded carrying our little people.

My husband's been known to carry our sons over rocks, uphill, downhill, in the blazing hot sun, around lakes, through the forest, and over the hill, to grandma's house we go.

We loved carrying our boys while we could. They're too big to carry now. They don't need to step on a crack to break their momma's back—they just need to jump into my arms.

Jesus knows you and I need to be carried too. He knew this before you were born. He welcomed you on this difficult terrain we call life, knowing you'd get tired and weak along the way. He's there to carry you. It brings him joy and fulfills his purpose as your rescuer, savior, and friend, when you go to him in and for all things.

When you feel as if you can't go on, you can't take another step, he's there. When you're overcome with weariness, loneliness, exhaustion, and crushing disappointment, that's when he shows up like the good friend he is. He will pick you up when you are down for the count. He will carry you not out of your circumstances, but through them, glued to your side each step of the way.

He longs to be your friend.

Peter, one of the first disciples of Jesus, said, "Cast all your anxiety on him because he cares for you."[6]

Because he cares for you.

Find your spot to meet with him, be it your couch or cave. Jesus sees you. He knows the burdens you have pressing in on your shoulders, weighing you down. He never intended you to carry your burdens alone. He said, "Come to me, all you who are weary and burdened, and I will give you rest."[7]

Now that's an exchange too good to pass up. Your restlessness for his rest. Your anxiety for his peace. Your weariness and worry for wonder found in him. Your disappointment for his friendship. Check, please.

Paul wrote a letter to a church, the Thessalonians, and in it, he reminded the people, "You are our glory and joy."[8] Jesus cares deeply for you and for me.

And because he is a good friend to us, we can be good friends to those around us.

Find your people. You'll be there for them and they'll be there for you too. You were made for friendship. Hush the lie that screams you don't need anyone, you've got this, nobody understands. You were not made to be an island.

Friendship is a gift from Jesus to help us walk through the difficulties and joys we face in our lives. Take him up on his invitation to be your friend. He cares for you!

That's for sure.

CHAPTER 8

Partners

Not long ago, a friend of mine gave me eye cream. She encouraged me to dab a tiny bit twice daily on the bags under my eyes—bags I didn't realize I had under my eyes, by the way, until I received the gift of eye-bag cream.

When I was all of nine years old, my grandma gave me a training bra on Christmas morning. What a letdown that was. A training bra? From Grandma? As if the gift itself wasn't embarrassing enough, we opened gifts as one big extended family that year, which meant my siblings, aunts, uncles, and cousins were eyewitnesses to my embarrassment.

We might not always be the best gift givers, but God is. He knows exactly what we need and he has already prepared ahead of time the greatest gifts ever to meet those needs.

In the few chapters preceding this one, we've breezed through a few of the gracious gifts God has given. These gifts—and many more we haven't mentioned—are intended to sustain us today.

God is good and loving. He knows this world is really hard. In his kindness and mercy, we've been given the gift of approaching him without inhibition at any time or in any place. We cannot visit the White House without a background check, an appointment, and a legit reason to be there. But we can approach Jesus at any time and find him ready and willing to hang with us for any and all reasons. We also reflected on the gift of healing Jesus extends to us and the wonderful, mysterious gift of his friendship.

I sincerely hope you've been able to see some of the good gifts he has given you to sustain you in your everyday moments through my personal sharing of what these gifts have looked like in my life. My stories are merely told as an attempt to relate to you and encourage you. I am in the trenches with you, dear friend.

God so freely gives us gifts to help us know him more. Knowing him helps us to understand who he made us to be. And his gifts not only help us know who he made us to be, but knowing him also helps us live well with those around us. He's available to us so that we can be available to others. He's forgiven us so that we can forgive others. He's a friend to us so that we can be a friend to one another.

The ways in which God gives us his presence and care far exceed what any book or mere words could ever capture. We're simply scratching the surface here by zeroing in on just a few ways he swoops down to be near and extends his compassion to us in transformative ways.

God far exceeds our every expectation and he loves to woo and wow us. He loves to amaze us and blow our minds with his goodness and glory. So, buckle up, Buttercup, and prepare to be amazed by one more gift God has poured out upon us like a cascading waterfall, to help us walk in the fullness of his design.

In his kindness and care, he has given you and me the gift of partnering with him to usher in justice, that is, to usher in his perfect order and the restoration of all things back to his original plan and design. By calling you and me his partners, Jesus invites us to participate with him in the restorative and redeeming work he is up to in the world. He's given each of us a role to play and a job to do in the greatest redemption story of all time—a story that ties the beginning to the end with thread woven throughout time, space, cultures, and generations. Partnering with Jesus to live according to his plan for justice and dignity for all transforms us, those around us, our neighborhoods, our communities, and even cultures at large.

———

My J Men know a thing or two about transforming. They have Transformer toys that change shape with little movements of their hands. The truck, helicopter, construction vehicles, and more transform and become standing robots with legs and arms. The J Men like to ball up on the floor in the fetal position and slowly unfold and stand to their feet as they transform into the most "epic robots ever."

Feel free to call me Captain Obvious here, but it is abundantly clear things are not as they should be in our world. I believe there's a longing in each one of us to transform that which has been distorted and mangled by the winds of chaos in the world into what we know to be orderly and right. Global issues such as human trafficking, war, hunger, disease, and depression are paralyzing realities. Closer to home perhaps, is the struggling single mom next door, the lonely widow down the street, the confused and anxiety-ridden teen stumbling through the day, the estranged married couple barely holding it together.

We long, on behalf of ourselves and others, for a life that will bring joy and peace, and not disruption, pain, and chaos. If it were as easy as balling ourselves up on the floor and then standing to transform our lives into what we believe is best for us, as well as for those around us, I think we'd find ourselves balled up on the floor often.

We don't always recognize it, but God has given us all we need to transform our worlds and, to the delight of my aging knees, it typically doesn't involve balling up on the floor.

Several years ago, I attended a conference where I heard International Justice Mission founder and CEO, Gary Haugen, respond to the reality of pain and suffering in the world. He said soberly, "You are God's plan A. There is no plan B." I felt like raising my hand and asking Gary to repeat what he said because, surely, I misheard. "What's that, Gary? I'm God's plan to change the world? This old lady with bags under her eyes? Me?"

If you've ever wondered if God has a sense of humor, well, now you know. His plan to restore the world back to the way he intended—back to that garden life, where people are seen as image bearers of God himself, designed with dignity and care—is us. It's you and me, Sparky. In his work to rescue, reconcile, restore, and renew, God invites us to join him in his mission to bring his design for all people into the world around us. Look no further than your mirror. The face staring back at you is the face of someone who God has fashioned and purposed for a specific job only you can do, to help bring heaven to earth and usher in rivers of justice for those around you.

And here's the best part: He does not wait for us to be perfect before he hands over a job for us to do. It's in the midst of our messy, busy, and chaotic lives that Jesus so graciously offers us real time-on-the-job training to join in the greatest global restoration project of all time. You don't have to earn that partnership with him. We aren't talking about a law firm here, where you have to prove for years that your name ought to be on a brass plaque on the door. Your name is on the door, right next to Jesus', the moment he calls you his. Partners, Jesus & Carrie. *Jesus & [your name here]*.

Often, I invite the J Men to help me with projects and domestic duties around the house. They help me bake cookies. They help with various paint projects around the house, they wash the car, and they care for the lawn. Sometimes their help makes a bigger mess for me to clean up, adding to my work. But as their mom, I love their help, mess or not, because I love having them near me. And I love seeing their faces beam with pride when handed the mixer, a washrag, or the mower. They run to get the cleaning supplies and can maneuver the vacuum like a boss.

I've noticed the more I invite them to help alongside me, the more their confidence in my love for them and their place in our family grows.

In similar fashion, out of God's love for us and his longing for us to be near him in all things, God has built into his plan for the restoration of the world partnership with us, his kids. He wants us right alongside him for the ride.

And as his partners, he's uniquely equipped us

for the jobs he's designed us to do in partnership with him.

Paul writes about this to the church in Rome. After eleven chapters of teaching the church in Rome more about who God is, and, therefore, who we are, Paul begins chapter twelve with the now-what application for our everyday life. Here's what he says, taken from *The Message* paraphrase:

> So here's what I want you to do, God helping you: Take your everyday, ordinary life—your sleeping, eating, going-to-work, and walking-around life—and place it before God as an offering. Embracing what God does for you is the best thing you can do for him. Don't become so well-adjusted to your culture that you fit into it without even thinking. Instead, fix your attention on God. You'll be changed from the inside out. Readily recognize what he wants from you, and quickly respond to it. Unlike the culture around you, always dragging you down to its level of immaturity, God brings the best out of you, develops well-formed maturity in you.
>
> I'm speaking to you out of deep gratitude for all that God has given me, and

especially as I have responsibilities in relation to you. Living then, as every one of you does, in pure grace, it's important that you not misinterpret yourselves as people who are bringing this goodness to God. No, God brings it all to you. The only accurate way to understand ourselves is by what God is and by what he does for us, not by what we are and what we do for him.

In this way we are like the various parts of a human body. Each part gets its meaning from the body as a whole, not the other way around. The body we're talking about is Christ's body of chosen people. Each of us finds our meaning and function as a part of his body. But as a chopped-off finger or cut-off toe we wouldn't amount to much, would we? So since we find ourselves fashioned into all these excellently formed and marvelously functioning parts in Christ's body, let's just go ahead and be what we were made to be, without enviously or pridefully comparing ourselves with each other, or trying to be something we aren't. (MSG)[1]

I love how God meets us exactly where we are. He doesn't ask us to learn a new trade, get another degree, or master a new challenge. He simply asks us to live our ordinary lives with a willingness to trust and yield to his way and restoration plan. Basically, get in your lane and do your thing. You've been chosen to play for Team Jesus. Your name is next to his on the door.

―――――――――

One of my favorite partner-up-with-God stories found in the Bible is the story of God inviting Moses to partner with him to free the Israelites from their captivity in Egypt. Moses had been a shepherd for forty years when God spoke to him. Prior to that season, during his first forty years, Moses had lived among the Egyptians. Therefore, Moses was eighty years old, and had already lived a lot of life, when God extended his invitation for partnership to Moses.[2]

Understandably, Moses panicked a bit and tried to talk God into choosing someone else for the job. Moses was overwhelmed. I've been there and I'm sure you have too. The idea that God would choose us, broken as we are, to join him is a lot to take in. But God knows you and I better than we will ever understand ourselves and he has a master plan our ant-sized brains simply cannot comprehend.

God had a plan for a great rescue of his people and Moses was the man he fashioned and equipped for the job. And God has a plan for me and you too. He has equipped every one of us with unique and specific gifts and experiences and wisdom that all point back to his good design of who he made us to be. And with those gifts comes an invitation for us to say yes to partnership with him in the restoration of all things.

And because God is so kind and because Jesus has authority over all things, even when we say yes to his call and events don't unfold the way we expect—and that's almost always—he is gracious and kind to remind us that he is the one who transforms, who initiates justice, and who brings the kingdom.

When he calls us to join him, he does not expect us to do what only he can do. He simply wants us along for the ride. In the same way I want my kids near me doing everyday activities, God wants you by his side as he carries out his restoration plan.

The Moses story is a great example that reminds us God invites us to partner with him, but ultimately, he is the one who rescues and restores.

Moses joined up with God and did exactly what God told him to do. He went to Pharoah and told him to let God's people go. Only, to Moses' surprise and frustration, Pharoah did not let the Israelites go. In fact, he made their lives even more difficult as slaves.

You can hear the frustration in Moses' voice as he reports back to God what took place. "Ever since I went to Pharaoh to speak in your name, he has brought trouble on this people, and you have not rescued your people at all."[3] Moses was frustrated because he had done exactly what God instructed him to do. He had been obedient. He said yes to partnership with God, and life got harder for the Israelites.

Has this happened to you? It has to me. I can think of several occasions where I was obedient to what I thought God was calling me to do, and then events I expected to take place just didn't go as I thought. In my experience, I almost always get frustrated first and then, as slow as molasses, I begin to see and understand that God is up to something good, something beyond what I can imagine.

God reminded Moses of his hand in the plan and basically instructed Moses to swallow a chill pill and trust him. God is the one who restores, who redeems, and who renews. He simply asks us to join him on mission.[4]

When the pandemic hit in 2020, I was working as the outreach pastor at a church in Huntington Beach, California. The church had been operating a food pantry at a local elementary school for a few years prior to the pandemic. But when everything closed, including the elementary school, there was no other choice but to move the food from the school to the church.

A handful of compassionate men and women from the church began to plan and work together to keep the pantry open to the community in a season when literally everything around us closed up shop. The church had even closed its doors to gathering for worship on Sundays. But people had to have food. Because of the quick action and care of these volunteers, the food pantry never missed a week of food distribution for the community.

For the first three months of the shutdown, this pantry was the only functioning pantry in a city of more than two hundred thousand residents, and it served more than three hundred families a week.

We could end the story here and it would be compelling. But it didn't stop there. This was not your average food pantry, which often requires proof of residence and, in some cases, proof of birth certificate, plus number of people living in the household, in order to receive food. Often recipients are given an ID number they must provide to get an allotment of food. And there are reasons behind these asks, of course. But in this season, as men and women who desired to serve the community out of the boatloads of goodness, grace, and generosity they themselves had received from God, these volunteers threw all that out the window. And instead, they handed out name tags so we could learn each other's names. In this way, we were able to treat one another with dignity and care that went beyond a bag of food.

The line was rather long at times, as you can

imagine when distributing bags of food to three hundred families, so volunteers began to serve coffee and water to the folks who stood in line. On many occasions music was playing, and the atmosphere was one of high energy and joy. And all of this during a time when so many were plagued with loneliness, fear, anxiety, and sadness.

It wasn't long before those volunteering and those receiving food knew one another on a first-name basis and began recognizing each other around town, at the gas station, on walks, at the bus stop. Walls that typically had divided this community because of language and cultural differences simply crumbled before our eyes. And in place of what so often divides us, community and friendship were formed.

Moses, in partnership with God, did eventually head up a massive rescue operation, leading an entire nation out of slavery. My friends in Huntington Beach, in partnership with God, led a once-divided community of people in need to a space thriving with love, dignity, and a beautiful picture of what it means to let justice roll.

Go about your ordinary life, do your thing, and rest in knowing Jesus wants us near to him in and for all things. His gift of partnership throughout this life is way better than eye-bag cream, training bras, or even the best gift you've ever received. He'll do the work of rescuing, restoring, and renewing. He simply wants us along for the ride.

That's for sure.

PART THREE

Go with Him

Drop the confetti. Send out the marching band. Bring out the chips and salsa. We've made it to the third and final part of *That's For Sure*.

Let's recap, because if you're anything like me, you set the book down a few days ago and need a quick refresher to help you dive back in.

So far, we've looked back to the creation story to get a clearer picture of who God made us to be, out of his bubbling-up and overflowing love. We can be sure God made us good because he is good.

And then we set out to discover just a few of the things Jesus gives us to get us through our days. Jesus has so kindly and graciously given us freedom to approach him at any time. We have freedom to call him friend and to partner with him to bring about transformation in this hurting world.

And as we'll see in the next few chapters, it's just as important to look back to the beginning to avoid entering full-on freak-out mode about tomorrow.

With so much chaos and destruction, doom and gloom swirling around us, globally and personally, how often do you wish you could build an indestructible fortress and hunker down inside with chips and salsa, protected from it all? I usually feel this way by 7 a.m. on any given day.

But, as the family of God, we have a living hope because Jesus lives. The tomb is empty. Jesus is living, and his Spirit is living and active in our lives, this very moment.

The Bible tells us Jesus is seated at the right hand of the Father.[1] He is busy reconciling to himself all things.[2] He's making all things new. He's restoring everything back to his original design and way. He's even praying to God about you, right now.[3] He's talking to God about you and cheering you on from heaven right now. He is busy working all things together for our good.[4]

In his beautifully written book *Gentle and Lowly*, author Dane Ortlund asks the question, "What if you heard Jesus praying out loud for you right now?" He goes on to declare, "Few things would calm us more deeply."[5]

This means pain, suffering, and life's trials are not the end. They are a season. The season will pass. Jesus is fixing all the brokenness and making sad things come untrue, right now.

In the family of God, no matter what tomorrow may bring, we have a living hope that is far greater than any present pain or suffering.[6] In today's world, that'll preach. Not only do we hope through our suffering, we rejoice in our suffering because our suffering drives us to the feet of Jesus. And in exchange for our grief and suffering, Jesus freely gives joy despite circumstance, peace despite pain, and rest in place of anxious worry.

Life's circumstances may not be what we want, yet we can be sure of the hope found in the one who promises to go "behind and before"[7] us and who says to us, "When you pass through the waters, I will be with you; and when you pass through the rivers, they will not sweep over you.

When you walk through fire, you will not be burned."[8]

In this third and final section of the book, we're going to focus on the living hope we have in Jesus and by his Spirit. We will find he is not far off. He is right beside us. He is knee-deep in the trenches of this life, right alongside us. And in him we have unshakable hope.

We'll spend the final four chapters reflecting on the incredible truth that our God longs to be known by us. He created us to be by his side in and through all circumstances. He has given us the gift of his Spirit, who is with us always. He is faithful and has proven throughout the ages that he can be trusted. He is the God we can absolutely be sure of, more than anything else in our lives. He is our rock to stand on. We have assurance and hope of tomorrow because he lives.

> Therefore do not worry about tomorrow, for tomorrow will worry about itself. Each day has enough trouble of its own. (Matthew 6:34)

Grab your chips and salsa. We're going to wrap up this book with a deep dive into a few more truths we can be sure of. Jesus wants us to know him. He can be trusted. He's with us in all things. And finally, he is our foundation upon which we stand. We can be sure of who he is and of his presence.

We can face tomorrow because he cares for us.

CHAPTER 9

Someone Who Cares

In the nineties, when pay phones were still in use, a Denny's diner server told me and a friend, "Here's a quarter—call someone who cares." I don't remember exactly why she said those words. But let's be real; we were at Denny's. Not exactly the place you go when you care about much of anything. I'm pretty sure caring has flown the coop if you find yourself seated in a Denny's booth.

Today, pay phones are ancient artifacts found in museums. But knowing someone cares is a shared longing of the human heart that transcends time, space, and culture.

A call-someone-who-cares moment unfolded in an adrenaline-charged scene in the Gospel of Mark.

After a long of day of teaching about what the kingdom of heaven was like, Jesus and the disciples climbed into a boat to cross to the other side of a lake. Jesus, likely exhausted from teaching all day, left the sailing to the disciples and went to the stern to take a nap. The Bible tells us Jesus was "sleeping on a cushion." His head rested on a cushion. He was relaxed. Jesus' long day of teaching however, was far from over. He was about to give the disciples a lesson in real-life application of his teachings—one that had much more to do with the storms in their hearts than it did with the physical storm that they experienced at sea.

Jesus must have been in a deep sleep, because as he napped, a storm began to rage and the disciples had to wake him up.

"Don't you care if we drown?"[1]

You can hear the fear and worry in their question.

In a moment when the disciples were absolutely afraid that they might die, Jesus slept.

There was a time in my life not too long ago when I wondered if Jesus was taking a nap while a storm raged and tossed about in my life and heart. My "don't you care?" moment arrived on my thirty-eighth birthday.

Not unlike the disciples pleading for Jesus to intervene and help them survive the literal storm, I had a come-to-Jesus talk with Jesus. I needed to clear some things up with him before a new decade rolled in like a hot Texas wind.

Knowing about Jesus was no longer enough. I needed to know that his words and ways were specific to me, Carrie Ellen. Did he really know my heart and care about my unique and individual desires? Believing he is good and present in day-to-day life is easy for me when it comes to someone else. But did I really know him to be good and did I believe he cared for me as an individual? I wasn't so sure.

I not only wanted to know Jesus cared for me deep down in the depths of my soul, I wanted to be absolutely sure he was concerned for me, in such a way that would change my day-to-day life. I wanted my weekly grocery runs and endless piles of laundry to have greater purpose because Jesus lives. And I wanted to know with confidence that he cared about the storm in my heart.

There are many metaphorical storms in life that drive us to wonder if Jesus is taking a snooze in the midst of our situation. For me, I was in the infertility boat with what felt like wave after wave of stress and worries that I might not have a second child crashing down, tossing me around. I was tired and I wanted out of the boat. And in the midst of my infertility storm, I desperately wanted to know Jesus cared. I needed to know and be absolutely sure he was indeed good, regardless of whether my family grew or remained a family of three.

The oldest J Man was four years old at this time and I wanted him to have a baby brother or sister to boss around. But after four years of struggling to get pregnant and failed help by the professionals, I was beginning to lose hope. I didn't know how much more of the longing for a baby I could take physically and emotionally. I had already endured a five-year fertility journey to have the oldest J Man.

Could I call Jesus good if I never held another baby who had my husband's brown eyes topped with my bushy eyebrows?

I felt lost in a sea of wondering if Jesus really knew my heart and knew exactly where I was. I was in the boat being tossed about, squinting my eyes in search of the lighthouse. I wondered if the lighthouse saw little ole me in the vastness of the sea. I was looking for my anchor, my footing, and my rock. Could I stand firm in my beliefs if the waves continued to crash?

_____

My desire to be seen and cared for in a deeply personal way by Jesus led me to take a look back.

Looking back and remembering when and how he had been good in my past helped fuel the flame of hope for whatever was next for me and my family.

In this season, I constantly asked Jesus to show up. I challenged him relentlessly to invade my life with his undeniable presence. Through persistent questioning—"Jesus, don't you care? Don't you care? Don't you care?"—I did come to see and know Jesus cared for me, Carrie, the woman who loves adventures and laughing and who is creeped out by all sorts of critters that walk the earth.

I set out to know for sure that Jesus knew me personally and cared about me through my infertility storm. My search led me to be convinced that not only did he know me, the real Carrie Ellen, but, in an unexpected plot twist, I also realized just how much he longs to be known by me and you.

He wants us to notice him at the grocery store,

in the car line, in the waiting room, in the stillness of the night, and in the deafeningly loud culture. He also wants us to see him in our boat in the middle of scary storms.

Isaiah 43 talks about the waters, rivers, and fire that will come our way. The struggle of life is real. And later in that chapter, we read that God will be with us through it all. He will make a way through the waters and be near to us, every step of the way. He is glued to our side throughout every moment and every hardship.

He's in the boat and he is telling a bigger story of his goodness and love in the midst of our individual storms and stories.

I came to better understand this mystery by returning to the beginning when God created all living things, especially Adam, the first dude on the planet. Looking back to the creation account helped me look forward and beyond my present storm.

In the same way it's always good to be home after time spent away, it's always good to go back to God—even better to never leave. God constantly calls us back to himself. When we go home, so to speak, and remember God's plan for us all, we find that after six days of creating, God took a break.

He stopped creating and rested.

Adam was spoken into existence on the sixth day. The seventh day was the end of the week for God, but it was the very beginning for Adam.

We aren't told what God and Adam did exactly on the seventh day, but I wonder if they simply enjoyed being together. God gave Adam a tour of the garden and the lowdown on how things worked.[2]

God wants to be known in the most relational ways. He did not create all the things and then peace out, mic drop, exit stage left, draw the curtain. He stepped into the story to be with Adam.

He steps into our stories to be with us too.

God is so concerned with you and me, he has gone overboard with the number of ways he's made it possible for us to know him. Namely, through creation, by his written word in the Bible, through community with one another, and, of course, in the person of Jesus—in all these ways, his words come to life in a way we can know relationally. Jesus came and "moved into the neighborhood" (MSG).[3]

In other words, Jesus boarded the boat.

The God who spoke all good and loving things

into existence knows us. He has us engraved on the palm of his hand.[4] He knows our every thought and move and he longs for us to know him too—not just to know about him from a distance, but to truly know him. To know what he cares about. To know what he loves, what his design and intentions for the world and for us are. He wants us to know his heart.

Creation, ancient Scripture, our current experiences, and the life of Jesus tell of God's relentless, unending love for us. All these things and more declare his desire to be known.

Knowing he's with us is what ushers in peace in the middle of the storm. Knowing him brings clarity and focus in the most confusing of times. Knowing him quiets the noise of the day and delivers rest. Knowing him snuffs out the wick of anxiety over tomorrow. Knowing him brings freedom and order in the chaos.

Jesus said, "I am the good shepherd; I know my sheep and my sheep know me."[5] Later, in John 10:27, Jesus continued, "My sheep listen to my voice; I know them, and they follow me."

My infertility struggle drove me to challenge Jesus on who he said he was and what his voice sounded like. I wanted to know the Good Shep-

herd and confidently follow him without inhibition, baby or no baby.

Jesus isn't afraid or turned off when we challenge him. In the Mark story, when Jesus woke
from his nap, he didn't rebuke the disciples for
waking him. He rebuked the wind and the waves.
He rebuked the storm that threatened his people.
But he didn't stop there. He had another storm to
calm: the storm in the hearts of those he deeply
cared about in the boat with him that day.

The disciples were guys who would've been in
their element in a boat on the lake. Some of them
were fishermen before they followed Jesus. They
were terrified in a place where they would've
typically felt very confident and comfortable. It
wasn't random that this story unfolded the way it
did in a setting the disciples were familiar with.

Jesus, again, concerned with the hearts of the
disciples, used the storm to help them see and
understand that his teachings were not simply
good ideas, practices, and traditions to follow, nor
were they just for other people. Rather, he gave
them a real-world experience to help them personally see and know that

1) they could trust his promises (he had said
   that they were going to the other side before

they stepped foot in the boat);

2) they could have complete confidence to face anything because he was present with them; and

3) they could experience peace despite the storm because Jesus has authority over all things (he illustrated this authority by napping as the storm raged).

We have his promise, his presence, and his peace in all circumstances.

Jesus cares too much about us to change our circumstances while leaving our hearts unchanged. Because he knows us individually, Jesus shows up in unique and personal ways that speak directly to us, in order to express his deep care for our souls in ways we understand.

———————

Little did I know at the time of my prayer on my thirty-eighth birthday that Jesus would do something similar in my life. He would use a space I felt confident and comfortable in to speak very clearly and to show up in my boat.

Before I became a mom to my oldest J Man, I traveled quite a bit. Traveling and spending time immersed in cultures other than my own was something that gave me great purpose. I spent time in Mexico, Malawi, the Democratic Republic of the Congo, Romania, and Moldova—beautiful countries with even more beautiful people. It was evident pretty early on in my travels that God wired me for the cross-cultural life. I flourished in contexts different from my own.

It was in this season of persistent asking for Jesus to speak directly to me that he made a way for me to travel to two gorgeous countries I had not yet experienced: England and Ireland. Yes, please. Sign me up.

While in England, I stayed with a friend, Iain, whom I had met while in Moldova in 2005. Seeing Iain again was a good reminder of what I had seen God do during our shared time in Moldova. On my final day in England, I toured the streets of London. I saw the church where theologian John Stott ministered. I rode the London Eye. I paid a visit to Buckingham Palace, fully expecting the queen to invite me in for tea. Of course, that didn't happen. I shrugged it off and kept walking.

As I walked, and in a way only he can do, I heard God's voice again. I remembered that he and I had done this before. We had walked together in a number of places. The memories of knowing without a doubt he was with me in Mexico, in the Democratic Republic of the Congo, and in all places I'd gone flooded my mind. He did see me. He did get me. He was with me.

The queen was too busy for tea with me that day, but I got something far greater: Jesus' undeniable promise, presence, and peace.

Later that day, I boarded the London Eye. From the top, I looked out over the city crawling with people from all over the world and I resolved that Jesus was good and he was very much concerned with me and my heart.

Only a few months after my trip to England, I flew to Ireland. On the same day the Lord Mayor of Dublin asked me who I was, I visited the breathtaking Cliffs of Moher. As I walked, I was overwhelmed by God's promise, presence, and peace again.

Standing on the edge of the massive cliffs, feeling very small, I was again convinced Jesus saw me. He knew my heart and he cared deeply for me. He again reminded me this was part of our song and dance and he was the lead.

How Jesus and the Spirit of God work is mysterious. But we can be sure Jesus is working. He willingly swoops into our story to sit next to us in the boat. He deeply cares for us and desires for us to know and to trust him.

David's words in the famous psalm speak to this incredible truth about God and his desire to be with us, especially in the storms: "Even though I walk through the darkest valley, I will fear no evil, for you are with me."[6]

Jesus hangs out in the valleys of this life. He's present in the difficult marriage. He can be found in the midst of a divorce. He's seated next to us in our disappointment and failure. He's not afraid to draw near in times of doubt, anger, trauma, and anxiety.

He sees suffering and he cares deeply.

He has compassion on us.

We can be sure he's in the storm with us and he's ahead of us. He's present in our tomorrow. When you and I wake in the morning and our own personal storms are still raging, he is there. He's at the next stop when we're aboard our hot-mess express. He's already arrived before we do. He's steps and leaps and bounds in front of us. He is all around us. There is nowhere we can go where he is not.

We have hope in the storm because we have him.

The disciples didn't yet understand who they had in the boat with them that day. Jesus could nap through the storm because he was creator of the winds and waves. He had then, and he has now, all authority over the wind, the waves, and the rain. He has all authority over the storms you face today.

He had authority over the lives of the men in the boat. He knew exactly what would happen next because nothing happens that doesn't happen by his command. Hence him resting his head upon the cushion as the storm raged on around the disciples. He was chill because he is in ultimate control. He knew the storm would not hurt the disciples. He was not at all alarmed by the storm in any way.

He also knew the storm would drive them to him, and because he cared so deeply for them, he was able to give them a real picture of what his kingdom was like. They had *heard* him teach about the kingdom all day. Now they *experienced* what life in the kingdom was like with King Jesus beside them.

Only a few years after the storm, Peter came face-to-face with death once more. His friend and fellow disciple James had been killed by King Herod and now Peter found himself arrested and in prison for telling others about Jesus. Herod planned to publicly try and kill Peter the next day. And Peter knew it. He was likely grieving his friend James and he must have been terrified for his life. And yet, the same Peter who had been in the boat and who woke Jesus to ask "Don't you care?" was the Peter who now, on the night before trial and death, slept between two soldiers in a prison cell.[7]

By this time, Peter had spent enough time near Jesus to recognize that, no matter what happened the next day, Jesus knew exactly where he was and what was happening to him. Peter didn't have to fear public trial or Herod. He slept between two soldiers in a prison cell because he trusted the King of Kings was the one in control.

Jesus' presence next to us in the boat is far greater than anything we can imagine.

In his kingdom, his kids know him, trust him, and are secure in his presence. Even in the middle of a storm.

In his abundant, radical mercy and grace that I will never fully understand, God answered the cry of my heart. He gave my family one more little J Man. I was first-trimester pregnant the day I visited and walked the Cliffs of Moher.

Throughout my lifetime, I have prayed a lot of prayers, asking Jesus for help in many ways. Oodles of my prayers remain unanswered—at least, not answered yet, in the ways I hope for. And it's only after walking with Jesus for a while (have I mentioned how grey my hair is?) that we begin to be grateful when he doesn't always give us what we want. Because if he did, we'd reduce him to a god who simply does what we want. Jesus has so much more in store for us than performing like a genie in a bottle at our command.

I don't understand it, but I know he's in the boat. And I know he can be trusted, no matter how violent or unpredictable the storm.

We don't need a quarter to call someone who cares. He already cares more for us than we can think or wrap our heads around.

That's for sure.

CHAPTER 10

Flying Under the Hood

When my husband, the Pilot, and I were first married, you could say I was as passionate about flying as I am about paying taxes. And yet, because my husband loves all things airplanes, and because I love my husband, I've learned more about the world of aviation than I ever imagined possible. I've even gone flying with him in the teeniest of aircrafts, arguably one designed for ants. This is love.

I don't know about you, but I require loads of faith to sit seat-belt-strapped to a tiny seat, aboard a hunk of metal designed to speed through turbulent skies. If my husband, who I know and trust, is the pilot, well, that's great: I can muster up enough courage to step aboard and take off. But zooming through the skies in an aircraft piloted by a stranger who sounds like a dinosaur roaring in an underwater tunnel when making cabin an-nouncements? That's how you throw this grey-frizzy-haired, middle-aged lady into a tailspin faster than the speed of sound.

If possible, I would step aboard only the planes my husband was piloting. I see the efforts he makes to ensure his upcoming flights are well thought-out and planned for. He's the guy you want flying your plane. He's meticulous, orga-nized, and focused. He plans well in advance for a flight. He studies weather patterns and reads the FAA guidance book for fun.

Through many years of dedication and hard work, he's earned the highest rating a pilot can receive, much like the PhD of the flying world. Traditionally outside the scope of what's required for a pilot, he also earned his aerobatic license. And not because he particularly enjoys flying a figure eight in the sky or purposely cutting the engine to enter a free fall. He willingly learned how to handle danger in the sky so that he could confidently recover if he ever did lose an engine midflight.

As if free-falling from the skies isn't scary enough, to earn his instrument rating license, he had to learn to fly what's called "under the hood."

You may know what this means, but when I first heard "under the hood," I imagined his head trapped literally under the hood of the plane.

Not that it's any better, in my opinion, but flying under the hood means wearing a large visor to block your line of sight and make you unable to see out the cockpit windows. The pilot flies solely by utilizing the instrument panel. All they can see is what's directly in front of them. It takes an incredible amount of faith to fly under the hood.

Here's the good news in this frightening situation: the pilot isn't in the cockpit alone when under the hood. Next to the pilot, in the right seat of the plane, is the safety pilot. The safety pilot's job is to be eyes on the skies. Phew. He's there as a guide and backup to the pilot. If the plane is headed into a hairy situation, the safety pilot is there to help guide the pilot away from any potential threat of danger. Flying under the hood means trusting the instrument panel and the guy next to you.

Knowing how to confidently fly the plane by the instruments alone is important for a pilot because it's easy to get disoriented in the skies and not know which way is up and which way is down. The instrument panel keeps the plane flying level and right side up. Yes, please and thank you.

An instrument panel on a plane is like water to a fish. If said instruments don't work properly, it's bad-news bears for all.

In the same way a pilot must rely on his instruments and a safety pilot, we too need a compass and a helper to guide us through this life.

We are people who like to see where we're going.

The problem with that, of course, is that none of us can see beyond where we are right now. We need flying-under-the-hood faith to get us through our days.

There's a passage in the Bible that says that without faith, it's impossible to please God.[1] To have faith in him is to trust that he can see what we can't and that's enough to follow him. Having faith is trusting in what is certain when what you see with your eyes is uncertain. It's putting one foot in front of the other when you have no idea what lies two or three steps ahead.

———————

While on a hike with my family one day, we found

ourselves in a literal fog. The path we hiked lines the cliffs of Crystal Cove State Park in Southern California. Ocean views from the cliffs are stunning. On clear days, we have spied with our little eyes pods of dolphins showing off their mad jumping skills. Just beyond the shore sits Santa Catalina Island, serving as the most beautiful backdrop to the breathtaking scene.

But on the morning of our hike, the fog was thick. From the cliffs, we were unable to see the water just below. We knew the water was there because we'd seen and experienced it countless times before. We could hear the waves crash and smell the ocean air, but we couldn't see it at all through the dense fog.

Living in faith is a lot like glaring into the fog and taking a step forward, trusting you'll find your footing, even when what you see with your eyes looks more like a cliff dive than a solid place to plant your feet.

The author of Hebrews wrote about this kind of faith: "Now faith is confidence in what we hope for and assurance about what we do not see."[2]

Faith is having limited or no visibility of what may be ahead *and* confidence to keep moving towards what we know to be true.

Speaking of Hebrews, it's fascinating to think that the men and women mentioned in the chapter of the book often referred to as the "great cloud of witnesses"[3] had faith to believe promises they would not experience the fulfillment of in their lifetime. And not because there was anything special or different about them. These were ordinary men and women.

Just like you and me, they struggled in life. They experienced pain and trauma. They lived mundane lives, and were going about their business as ordinary people when God encountered them in some way. They resolved to trust in God in the middle of their ordinary lives and their faith in him led them to some extraordinary experiences.

Abraham is one guy among the great cloud of witnesses who was living his ordinary life when God struck up a conversation with him. Abraham was well established, married, owned a farm full of livestock, and by the world's standards in his day, was a very successful dude. But he was, as the Bible describes, so old, he was *as good as dead*[4] and he and his wife Sarah didn't have any kids.

God said some shocking things to old man Abe. Things like, you're not only going to have a son in your old age, but you're going to be the father of more kids than the number of stars in the sky. Not only will you be the patriarch of this huge family, but you're going to be blessed, they're going to be blessed, and everyone is going to be blessed to bless. That's a lot of blessing. Bless.

Good ole Abe didn't receive much more than that when God met him that day. God simply said, I am God. Go to the place where I will show you. You're going to be a dad, old man, and I'm going to be with you. And Abe said OK, packed up his stuff, and went on his way, with wife Sarah and their entire household of workers and livestock. They had no idea where God would lead them, they simply trusted his lead.

Then there's Noah. Noah was going about his ordinary life in a dry desert land in a culture of people who had turned away from God. After Noah had lived many years in a wicked and perverse culture, God filled Noah in on a storm that would soon roll in and flood the earth. And the Bible tells us that Noah believed the God who told him about the imminent rain that would cover the earth. Noah was committed to building a boat without a rain cloud in sight. By faith in what God said alone, Noah built a boat.

Jacob was promised he'd call the promised land

home, but he didn't get to stay there. In fact, at the time of his death, the promised land was experiencing a famine. He trusted in God's promise, knowing it was greater than what he could and would see for himself in his lifetime. He trusted that God was the architect of an eternal promised land, a land he wouldn't come to know until his death.

Faith in God reminds us there is more to the story. It's trusting that something greater is taking place behind the scenes. It's believing that our current circumstances aren't the end-all, not by a long shot. What lies ahead and beyond the horizon is worth striving for. It's worth putting one foot in front of the other and marching onward towards. Even in zero visibility conditions. Faith is acknowledging the current reality stinks and trusting it will pass because God says it will. Faith is hope for what is yet to come.

Faith is believing you will be healed after a cancer diagnosis. Healing may come in this lifetime. Or it may be in the yet-to-come. But it will come.

Faith is believing we will be reunited with our loved ones who are no longer with us.

Faith is having eyes to see that our current circumstances, painful as they may be, are fleeting and a new day is dawning.

Faith is believing Jesus is standing with a wayward child, ready to swoop in and to rescue, redeem, and return that which was lost.

Faith is believing cries for our lost loved ones are sowing deep roots that God will one day harvest and restore.

When what we see around us feels empty and tired, faith is the on-ramp to a highway of hope for a brighter day.

I can't think of a more fitting example of this kind of life-changing faith and hope than what my friend Christy is up to in an unlikely place. Christy co-owns a pottery studio in Fresno, California. Often the butt of jokes, Fresno is located in the Central Valley of California. It's surrounded by farmland that produces a large amount of the country's nut, dairy, and fruit supply. If you pay a visit in the summer, when the temps run in the triple digits, bring a clothespin for your nose. The stench from the surrounding farmland is enough to smack you into tomorrow. I know this because I lived in the boonies farmland area of Fresno as a teenager in the 1990s. Cue the tiny sympathy violin.

Unfortunately, gangs are a reality in some areas

of Fresno and with that comes drugs, human trafficking, and a high crime rate. The foster care system in Fresno is bursting at the seams, desperate for something to give.

And it's within this setting that we find the Good Dirt Pottery Studio.[5]

Christy and co-owner Jorden believe shaping clay can help shape the world. As you enter through the glass front doors of the studio, a variety of handcrafted pottery pots and vases invite you to come in and relax. Positioned along wooden wall slats in the entryway of the store, in large all-cap black letters, a sign reads, EVERY ONE NEEDS GOOD DIRT TO GROW.

The studio has a room with a large wooden table, perfect for groups to gather around and exercise their creativity on with a slab of clay. Adjacent to the long table is an area equipped with pottery wheels for those who prefer to throw their clay on the wheel and spin it into shape.

The Good Dirt Pottery Studio is welcoming and warm, and the owners and staff even more so.

Christy and Jorden believe that when youth and adults are given space to dream, create, and cultivate, things change. Transformation takes place. The pottery instructors give everyone an opportunity to get their hands dirty and to create something unique to them. They strive to help every person who walks through the door see their worth and dignity. And they do it with simple dirt and clay.

While the studio is open to the general public, they also offer classes for the vulnerable, such as Fresno's foster youth population. They desire to make space for those whose circumstances are sad and to help them unlock hope for a different way.

Sometimes we just need a little dirt, and space to get our hands dirty, for hope to take root and sprout into something beautiful.

Christy is a hero of mine. She makes Fresno cool, but more than that, she spends her life at the pottery studio and beyond, planting seed after seed of intentionality, hospitality, and goodness by her welcoming and friendly presence. She makes everyone feel like they are the greatest thing to hit planet Earth and they are valuable and wanted. She's flinging hope around like she's made of it, because, well, she is.

Christy also knows discouragement, because what's in her line of sight doesn't always align with what she believes Jesus is up to. Some days, it's easy for her to question if her efforts with the studio are producing fruit and changing lives like she hopes. Despite this, she keeps showing up and doing her very best to trust her safety pilot. She operates out of believing he is next to her in all things and while she can't see the end result of the studio, she trusts Jesus can. She believes he is writing a different story for the youth of Fresno and in faith, she's following his lead.

Christy's faith has given her hope for something greater than what she can see. That hope led her to action, action that's changing lives. But the reality is, Christy will likely never know the impact the Good Dirt Pottery Studio is making and will continue to make upon the community.

This is exactly what faith is. We simply cannot understand fully what God is up to. He doesn't give us the answers or invite us to peek behind the scenes and see a picture of what he's doing. He simply asks us to go to the place where he will show us.

In the same way the safety pilot is able to help my husband when he's flying under the hood, God invites you and me to copilot through life *with* him. Sure, it's risky business and full of unknowns, but it leads to an adventure like no other.

How often are we blind to the presence of God

near us because our focus is on what we cannot see, rather than upon *who* we know?

It takes a crazy amount of trust to follow a God we cannot see and to believe his promises whose results we may never experience in our lifetime. He's never not fulfilled a promise and he's not going to start now. You are safe with him. Walk with him when you're blinded by the fog.

Faith is trusting in Jesus when everything around is spinning. Jesus is our safety pilot throughout all of life's experiences. We keep our eyes glued to him and he will strengthen us to press on no matter how uncertain we may feel.

Strap your seat belt on and know you can trust the pilot.

That's for sure.

CHAPTER 11

The Good Guide

It was dark.

Real dark.

My boys and I walked as near to each other as possible without stepping onto one another's feet.

We walked along a path that wove its way around a tall-grass meadow. We continued across a wooden bridge that hovered above a calm lake and through a wooded area boasting pecan trees and a variety of shrubs. What little light we did have was all that remained from a gorgeous sunset.

Without much light, the sounds of the night were accentuated and amplified. We heard deer rustling in the meadow and the song of birds, each one unique from the other. Frogs croaked in the waters nearby and the sounds of crickets and other insects made me thankful for the dark. Bugs are a hard pass for me. Had I been able to see these loud creatures, I might have caused a scene.

Thankfully, we were not alone, nor lost. We had lived in the area only a few short months and were in search of adventure in our new town. A night hike seemed like a great way to jump in and explore our new digs.

Traveling with a group of people, we were led by a guide. We could hardly make out the guide's silhouette up ahead in the dark, but we knew he was there. As he forged the way, we made sure to keep up and not fall behind. No one has time to get attacked by creepy creatures in the night, which I was certain beyond all certainty would happen to us if we didn't keep in step with our guide.

The group guide, a grandfatherly man in his seventies, had an obvious love and respect for the outdoors. He kept us moving forward with enthusiasm and wisdom. A nature center volunteer for many years, he knew the layout of the land. He knew when to tell us to not use the railing as we crossed the bridge, because while it appeared to be supportive, it was not. He told us to walk one foot in front of the other down the center of the bridge to avoid the danger of stepping off the side and plunging into the cold waters below. Waters that were home to snakes, by the way. You can bet your spring hat I took heed of his warning.

Mr. Guide had a flashlight, but he only turned it on to point out interesting characteristics of various trees and plants along the way. Other than that, he led us in complete darkness. We had no choice but to listen for his voice and follow his instruction carefully for the duration of the roughly two-mile-long hike.

Following Jesus can feel a lot like one long night hike. None of us knows what lies ahead and what's around the bend. We have no idea what tomorrow holds, the phone call we may receive, or the good or the bad news that may come our way. But we can be absolutely certain we have a trail guide and he is leading us home, to the place where there is no suffering, no pain, no animosity, no hurt, and no shame.

After the resurrection of Jesus and before he ascended to heaven, he comforted his followers by letting them know his Spirit was coming and that when the Spirit came, he would guide them. He would comfort them. He would lead them and they would never be without his presence. Jesus cares too much about us to leave us without his help.

When we say yes to Jesus, we receive the same

gift of the Spirit today. The Spirit of God is the good guide who patiently directs us one day at a time. He moves. He leads. He nudges. He directs. He comforts. He cares. We are never alone and left to figure out our own way. The Spirit of God is always nearby.

This is truth we can be absolutely sure of because it's on repeat throughout the Old Testament. The Israelites would get off track and cry out to God for help. He would help them. The Israelites would get off track again and God would rescue them again. This pattern repeated over and over again throughout the Old Testament narrative.

No matter how far they swerved off course, there was no distance great enough to prevent God from rescuing them and setting them back on the right path—a path that every time, always, without fail, led to him.

Isaiah 58 is just one example of many passages throughout the Old Testament where we read about God's people losing their way. And as a result, they began to grossly misunderstand God and the freedom and flourishing he had designed for them.

And because time after time God faithfully sticks by his people, he met them in their wandering and reoriented them back to himself and to the type of living he had purposed and fashioned them for. He picked them up and set them back on course. He dusted them off and reminded them who they were as his loved and chosen people. And he reminded them of his heart and what concerned him most: their hearts and the hearts of those around them.

God graciously outlined the path he had set before them, a path that bends and curves throughout all types of pain and suffering and one in which he walks with them. He urged his people to move in step with him and to spend themselves on behalf of the poor, to set the oppressed free, and to supply others with basic needs.

And he reminded them that following him leads down a path towards purpose, joy, and contentment. God tells them that as they follow him, their night will shine like the noonday sun. He assures them that they will be like a well-watered garden and will find their joy in his presence along the way.

We don't mean to veer off path. It's something that happens slowly and most often without us being aware we're moving in a direction that differs from God's best for us. We can feel certain we are following the way of God, when, in fact, we are merely going through the motions of following him, like dead men walking, and not actually living in the fullness of the life he has designed.

We are people created to keep in step with the Spirit of God.

When he moves, we move.

When he stops, we stop.

As is the case with any relationship, it takes time to learn the movements and actions of someone else. We learn how to notice the movements of the Spirit of God as we spend time with him.

Time spent with him reading the Bible, or in creation that has his fingerprint all over it, helps us to know him. Spending time in community with others who share faith in him also helps us learn who he is and what he's like. And over time, we begin to recognize his prompts, the gentle nudge or the sounding alarm.

We won't get it right every time and that's okay.

The best news ever for you and me is that regardless of when and how often we find ourselves off course, the Spirit is always with us. We cannot venture too far beyond or ahead and out of reach of his grasp and care. There is nowhere out-of-bounds beyond his reach.

As he did time and time again for his people throughout some excruciatingly trying times recorded in the Old Testament, he continues to show up with mercy and grace, abounding in love, in order to lead us back onto the path.

He's the night-hike guide we desperate need to help us navigate throughout life. And as we keep in step with him, we discover the promises he says will be ours in Isaiah 58 and so many more places throughout his Word.

In Genesis 5, we find a mysterious story about a guy named Enoch.[1] Enoch became a dad at age sixty-five and then, we are told, Enoch walked with God for three hundred years. This was back in the day when people lived exceptionally long lives.

We aren't told any more about Enoch's life or what he endured as he walked with God. We don't get the juicy details of his long life. But we know Enoch lived in the pre-flood world when people were selfish and corrupt and nasty wicked. Yet, despite living in an evil world, Enoch walked with God. That's it. This simple truth is all we know of Enoch's life. We don't know the hilltop moments or the low valley seasons he likely endured given the dark culture he lived in. All we know is he walked with God.

I desperately want to walk with God. Strike that. I desperately *need* to walk with God.

Far too often I have wandered away from his presence, believing I knew enough or I had experienced enough, and I have strayed from his guiding lead. I've walked off the path he has set before me because of my pride and ignorance. I've faltered many times and lost my footing along the way. I've relied too much on the opinions of others and not enough on what he had to say. I've run too far ahead in excitement, without slowing enough to consider his timing. I've forgotten that his ways are not mine and he is telling a much bigger and broader story than I could even begin to imagine.

In his kindness, Jesus isn't upset, annoyed, or disappointed when we find ourselves drifting from the paths he's designed for us to walk in. He's patient with us. He lovingly stands beside us. He goes with us in our pursuits of what we think we ought to do while continually whispering, "Come, follow me." He's generous with his time and draws from a bottomless bank account of patience and understanding, care and kindness.

When left to our own judgement on what we come face-to-face with in this life, we may too easily find ourselves on a slippery slope that moves us off path. Our hearts were designed to trust solely in the Lord.[2] Trusting in our own hearts and what we think is right leads us down the wrong path every single time.[3]

———————

When my parents moved to Texas from California, my mom, the J Men, and I followed close behind my dad and brother in their Penske moving truck throughout the three-day drive. Somewhere along the way, we stopped at a rest stop. (By the way, why are they called rest stops? There is to be no resting on a long drive, people. This is a pit stop. Get out. Take care of your business and get your tushy back in the car faster than two shakes of a lamb's tail. We have fifty-six thousand more miles of open road to conquer before sundown. Chop, chop.)

When it was time to leave the rest stop, I decided to wait for my brother and dad to pass in the Penske so I could follow them. The Penske passed by us a little bit faster than I thought my brother would've been driving, but I figured he was as eager as I was to get back on the road. I hit the pedal to the metal and followed close behind.

About an hour had passed when he pulled off the freeway again. Only this time, there was no rest stop in sight. Why was he pulling off again so soon? I followed close behind as he made a left off the off-ramp and then a right onto a tiny side street in what appeared to be a ghost town. The only sign of life was a lone elderly man wearing a cowboy hat and snakeskin boots, who walked across the street. Were we on the set of a Clint Eastwood Western movie?

My mom and I rolled up just a few feet next to the driver's side window of the Penske, ready to shoot arrows of questions aimed at my brother and dad. The door to the Penske opened and a guy who was definitely not my brother stepped out. He was as shocked as we were and he stared at us in confusion. I hit the gas pedal once again to get us out of Dodge.

Unfortunately for us, we were on a dead-end street. As if we weren't embarrassed enough (and a little bit frightened), we had to flip a U-turn and drive back by stranger-danger man again. We waved sheepishly and got out of there NASCAR fast.

We made our way back to the freeway and onto the on-ramp just as my dad and brother drove by in *their* Penske. We merged in behind them just as if we had been there all along. Sweet relief was had by all—maybe even more than was had at the rest stop just an hour before, if you catch my drift.

At the hotel later that night, my dad and my brother told us that border patrol had done a cursory check of the Penske trucks at the rest stop. From where we sat in the car, my mom and I hadn't been able to see any of this because of other large trucks blocking our view. The border patrol agents were in hot pursuit of someone driving a Penske truck. I don't know for certain, of course, but I wonder if we inadvertently ended up following bad news.

Who we follow matters.

We won't always get it right, but we can be absolutely certain the Spirit of God is with us in and through every bend and curve of life that may come our way. When we follow him, we will feel peace in our heart. We can trust his lead.

He's with us to comfort us, be near us, and go with us.

We are never alone.

Our adventurous night hike was a simple reminder of the importance of heeding the words and wisdom of the guide. We follow where the Spirit of God leads because he's ultimately leading us home and to the renewal of all things. Jesus said he's preparing a place for us.[4] In the meantime, while we wait with confident and expectant hope for that day, we follow the Spirit of God, who leads and guides and comforts along the way.

Just as Mr. Night-Hike Guide kept our group close-knit for the duration of the hike, our God is a God who keeps us close. As his kids, we are kept near and surrounded by him and his protection. Nothing can remove us from his loving care, not even when we find ourselves a little lost. This is when he comes rushing in to save, protect, wipe the dust off our worn-out and tired selves, and champion us onward.

He leads.

We follow.

No matter how dark the path may appear, we have a good guide who is with us.

That's for sure.

CHAPTER 12

Joy and Hope

I'll shoot straight with you and let you know that I am not exactly a fan of the feathered beast. So it goes without saying, I was grief-stricken to learn I'd be rooming with a tiny bird boasting green feathers and beady little eyes during a stay in Moldova in 2005.

To the near end of me, the little green bird was cage-free. He had freedom to flap his creepy wings and fly about throughout the apartment. But I did not want to be a high-maintenance, sissy American, so I mustered up some courage and told myself to be grateful for the hospitality. And I was truly grateful. Except during breakfast, when the foul fowl—see what I did there—would nosedive for a bird bite of my morning toast.

I tried not to flinch in fear too obviously, because seated across the table from me was my kind and gracious hostess, Tatyana. Tatyana was completely unfazed as her pet bird zoomed around our heads. Her smile was warm and she sat calmly with her hands folded in her lap.

Tatyana's hands told quite a story.

In the evening, the bird was caged and Tatyana shared some of her experiences living as a Christian in an oppressive communist culture during the 1980s. Because we spoke different languages, Tatyana would call her son on the tan phone that hung on the wall above the round table for two in her kitchen. He lived in a neighboring country, Romania.

Tatyana would speak to her son in Romanian and then pass the phone to me so I could hear him kindly relay her stories in English. She sat across from me at the tiny table and grinned from ear to ear as her son translated unbelievably difficult stories of Tatyana's reality during the oppressive and extremely anti-Christian time she endured.

As he spoke, Tatyana showed me deep scars that ran across the palms of her hands.

In 1985, Tatyana and her friends were in the process of building a church. They were given permission to continue building the church, however, they were told they would be unable to use building equipment to get the job done. But hearing this only fueled their passion and commitment to build the church. The scars on her palms were from smoothing concrete by hand.

At the time of Tatyana's storytelling, I was unaware of what she had planned for us the following day.

The next morning, we ate our breakfast toast and I dodged the bird dives once more. Then we left the apartment and I sighed in relief to finally have a minute away from the bird. Tatyana and I boarded a taxi van for the city. From our stop, we walked a few blocks to a large church building. As we entered, I followed Tatyana around as she joyfully greeted several people. It wasn't long before I realized this was a reunion.

It was the twentieth anniversary of the completion of the church, the church on which Tatyana had used her hands to smooth the concrete. The two hundred or so in attendance were her friends who labored alongside her to complete the church in the midst of persecution. These men and women shared stories of being separated from loved ones, and being beaten and hurt because of their faith in Jesus.

But this was not a reunion to remember the

pain and suffering, although that was a very real part of their stories. Rather, this was a joyful reunion of people praising Jesus because of his faithfulness and goodness to them in the midst of their pain.

Stories were told of Bibles and children's books about Jesus being confiscated and trashed. In their place, communist literature was distributed. And then the room erupted in laughter and praise as they told story after story of how they would write Bible verses they had memorized and encouraging notes to one another within the pages of the communist books. And they got away with it because as long as the covers were untouched, the soldiers didn't bother to look at the content inside.

I sat next to Tatyana in complete awe. She beamed from ear to ear, listening to her friends share. She cried. She laughed. And she raised her scarred hands in praise to the One who was with her through all the experiences and emotions.

Later than night, the bird was caged and we called Tatyana's son because I had questions. I asked Tatyana if she had any regrets about following Jesus when it meant increased suffering for her, her family, and those around her. I asked her, if communism were to enter into Moldova with the same intensity again, would she flee?

She smiled and ran her fingers across the scars on her palms and she told me she had no regrets. Her smile grew as she went on to say that the most joyful times of her life were also the most painful. She would absolutely endure pain all over again if it meant she could know joy like she had during that time once more. She credited her joy to experiencing the Spirit of God, undoubtably close to her throughout that season.

Tatyana showed me through her scars and her stories that having joy has little to do with circumstances and everything to do with who we know.

She kept her eyes fixed on Jesus and the promises of his Word. She found her strength in knowing the Spirit of God was with her and her good guide through tough terrain. God was faithful to keep his promises to be with Tatyana and her friends through a difficult time. And in the midst of the chaos and suffering, they experienced genuine joy.

This was the kind of joy Jesus' brother James wrote about when he said, "Consider it pure joy, my brothers and sisters, whenever you face trials of many kinds, because you know that the testing of your faith produces perseverance."[1]

James reminds us that Jesus takes the crummy and turns it into cheers.

Pain is given purpose.

Peace is graciously given to us in the midst of persecution.

Suffering reaps a harvest of joy.

Nothing is wasted with God.

———————————

I met Karen in Malawi in 2008. Karen was a young woman who walked with me and a couple hundred teenagers from camp to nearby Lake Malawi every day for a week. Karen was full of joy. She was tall and thin, with a contagious smile. She was great with the teens and I admired her gentle yet firm way with them. On our final day of walking the mile or so to the lake, I asked Karen to tell me her story. I was not prepared for what she shared.

When Karen was just a child, her uncle murdered her father over a family dispute tangled up in witchcraft. Karen, her younger siblings, and her mother had no other choice but to rely on her uncle for support. As you can imagine, she endured years of trauma and abuse under his care. Eventually, her uncle died of malaria, leaving her family without a caretaker yet again. Because Karen was the oldest, she had to drop out of school and find a job to support her mom and siblings.

Karen was such a delight on our daily walks to the lake, I would have never guessed she had such a painful past.

I asked Karen where her joy came from. Her reply? "God is faithful to me."

Without Jesus, Karen's story doesn't make sense.

Joy is a universal longing of the soul. In American culture, we have many ideologies regarding what brings about a joyful life. Often, we are told to do what makes us happy or feels good and right to us, and there we will find our joy.

This sounds similar to the lie the serpent in the Garden used to deceive Eve. He convinced her to believe she could decide for herself what was good and lovely for her. The truth is, only God can decide what's good and what's good for us. And the more we believe we are capable of determining what is good and right for us, the greater our spiral down into more depravity, more confusion, and life completely void of joy.

Tatyana had the truth of God's message of love, nearness, and hope written on her heart before times got tough. When the persecution came, she didn't panic. She remained. And in a supernatural and unexplainable way only God can orchestrate, she was given exactly what she needed in order to endure through that season. Her endurance shaped her character, grew her faith, and produced inexpressible joy. She knew her suffering was temporary. Conversely, her assurance of the hope she stood firm upon was eternal.

Peter, who suffered greatly for his faith in Jesus, reminds us that Jesus freely gives us joy in the suffering.[2]

Peter wrote words of encouragement to fellow Christians who were being persecuted and who suffered greatly because they called Jesus their Lord and King. They followed Jesus and his ways and lived under his rule and reign first and before any earthly kingdom and rule.

Their hope was secured and anchored in the truth of the gospel message: Jesus lives and our allegiance is reserved for him alone.

When we use the word *hope* today, we think of it more like a wish: something we aren't certain of but sure would like to be true. We hope it's sunny tomorrow. We hope we win the game later. We hope we get that college acceptance letter. We hope we get the job.

But the hope we read about in the Bible, specifically the living hope Peter encouraged his people with,[3] means something we can be absolutely sure of. The Greek word for hope is *elpis* and it means to have absolute, expectant confidence. We can be absolutely sure Jesus will do what he says he will do. He is faithful to keep his promises and because of that we have a living hope we can bank on no matter how dark or troubling our circumstances.

In this world, we will suffer. The trials of life will come. Personally, I hope they don't involve communism, witchcraft, or flighty green birds. But the truth remains: with feet firmly planted upon our foundation of Jesus and his Word, he will sustain us through whatever comes our way. He will walk through it with us.[4] It's who he is and it's what he does.

He is our living hope.

Like Tatyana, I want my scars that the struggles of life have caused to be turned into praise to my God. Only a good and loving God can take our pain and turn it into joy.

God loves us. He wants us close to him, just like he made Adam and Eve to be in the Garden. He wants to protect, surround, and defend us. This is the love of a Father for his children. The Bible is God's way of telling us what he's like. Jesus is God's way of personally showing us what he's like. The Holy Spirit is God's way of guiding us, like a light, to grow closer and closer to God. He is our compass throughout the journey of life.

And in him we find our joy.

You are loved.

That's for sure.

May the God of hope fill you with all joy and peace as you trust in him, so that you may overflow with hope by the power of the Holy Spirit. (Romans 15:13)

Conclusion

My oldest son has taught me a whole heap about the art of building a firm foundation. He loves to build and create with Legos. Early on in his childhood Lego-building career, he learned quickly that regardless of what he was building, he needed to begin with a firm, solid foundation. All attempts to build upon anything other than on a solid foundation piece is useless. A Lego crash, with launching pieces flying everywhere, is inevitable. Your feet will hate you later as they find every piece of Lego shrapnel strewn around the house.

The Word is God's message of love for us. The Word is our foundation we grow and build upon.

The Word is an anchor for the soul and a compass that always points us home to the Father. Until we get there, the Word reminds us God is for us.[1] The Word reminds us God is near.[2] The Word reminds us God is kind.[3]

As Peter set out to help the Christians in his

day to stay alert, to be disciplined in the Word, and to keep their eyes fixed upon Jesus, I pray these stories and words have encouraged you to stick close to the good God who cares so deeply for you. He has proved his love for you by sending his Son Jesus to die.

Jesus, so fierce is his love for you, willingly stepped into an angry crowd, endured a beating so bad that he was hardly recognizable, and ultimately died upon a cross. He stepped into the greatest pain in order to free us from ours. The Bible tells us it was for the joy of setting us free and giving us eternal life that he conquered death and raised us to new life.

There is nothing he cannot do for you.

I pray you find your comfort, hope, and joy in the best gift ever, the mysterious Spirit of God, who delights in leading you home, where you belong.

That's for sure.

Acknowledgments

Pilot, thank you for still making me laugh like no one else can.

J Men, I have no greater joy than being your mom. I am so proud of who you are and the men you are becoming. Thank you for being my greatest teachers of the love God has for us all. I love you much, much, much.

Mom and Dad, thank you for being supportive and for loving our family so well. Thank you for sharing the love of Jesus with me by your words and actions. Your love and care will bless our family for generations to come.

Kim, thank you for your care and commitment to helping me see this project through! I am a fan. And I am eternally grateful for you. Thank you.

Bob, thank you for cheering me on throughout the writing process. Your kindness is unmatched.

Notes

Introduction

1. 3 John 1:4.

2. John 15:5.

Chapter 1: Who Are You?

1. Genesis 1:31.

2. Alistair Begg and Sinclair B. Ferguson. *Name above All Names*. Wheaton, Illinois: Crossway, 2013.

3. James 1:17.

4. Colossians 1:17.

5. John 14:6.

6. Isaiah 43. The whole chapter is a beautiful reminder of how God loves us and is with us always.

Chapter 2: The Song and the Story

1. John 1:1–2.

2. Genesis 1:31.

3. Job 38:7.

4. Sally Lloyd-Jones. *The Jesus Storybook Bible*. Grand Rapids, Michigan: Zonderkidz 2007.

5. Sandra Thurman Caporale, "My Very Breath," Digging Deeper Media, February 17, 2022, https://diggingdeeper.net/2022/02/17/my-very-breath.

6. Psalm 8:3–4.

Chapter 3: Protected

1. Psalm 18:2.

2. Hebrew: ganan (gaw-nan'). Strong's Concordance, Bible Hub, https://biblehub.com/hebrew/1598.htm.

3. Hebrew: teba.(ta-va). Strong's Concordance, Blue Letter Bible, https://www.blueletterbible.org/lexicon/h8392/kjv/wlc/0-1.

Chapter 4: Family Business

1. Luke 8:40–56.

2. Hebrew: gâ'al (gaw-al'). *Strong's Concordance*, Blue Letter Bible, https://www.blueletterbible.org/lexicon/h1350/kjv/wlc/0-1.

3. Christopher J. H. Wright. *The Mission of God*. Downers Grove, Illinois: InterVarsity Press, 2006.

Chapter 5: Crash

1. Mark 10:14–16.

2. Matthew 11:28.

3. Hebrews 12:2.

Chapter 6: Drop Your Jar and Run

1. John 4:1–42.

Chapter 7: Couch Coffee Chats

1. *Friends*, television series, created by David Crane and Marta Kauffman, 1994–2004.

2. Dominic Done. *Your Longing Has a Name*. Nashville, Tennessee: W. Publishing Group, an imprint of Thomas Nelson, 2022.

3. Genesis 2:18.

4. Jonathan Evans, "When Misery Becomes Ministry," December 15, 2022, in *Viral Jesus with Heather Thompson Day*, podcast, https://www.christianitytoday.com/ct/podcasts/viral-jesus/jonathan-evans-fighting-your-battles.html.

5. Psalm 55:22.

6. 1 Peter 5:7.

7. Matthew 11:28.

8. 1 Thessalonians 2:19–20.

Chapter 8: Partners

1. Romans 12:1–6, *The Message*. Colorado Springs, CO: NavPress, 2018.

2. Exodus 2:11–4:17.

3. Exodus 5:23, Moses tells God what Moses did.

4. Exodus 6:1–8, God tells Moses what God will do.

Part Three: Go with Him

1. Colossians 3:1.

2. Colossians 1:20.

3. Romans 8:33–34; Hebrews 7:25.

4. Romans 8:28.

5. Dane Ortlund, *Gentle and Lowly*. Wheaton, Illinois: Crossway, 2020.

6. 1 Peter 1:3–12.

7. Psalm 139:5.

8. Isaiah 43:2.

Chapter 9: Someone Who Cares

1. Mark 4:35–41.

2. Genesis 2.

3. John 1:14, *The Message*. Colorado Springs, CO: NavPress, 2018.

4. Isaiah 49:16.

5. John 10:14.

6. Psalm 23:4a.

7. Acts 12:1–6.

Chapter 10: Flying Under the Hood

1. Hebrews 11:6.

2. Hebrews 11:1.

3. Hebrews 11.

4. Hebrews 11:12.

5. The Good Dirt Pottery Studio, https://gooddirtpotterystudio.com.

Chapter 11: The Good Guide

1. Genesis 5:21–24.

2. Proverbs 3:5–6.

3. Jeremiah 17:9.

4. John 14:3.

Chapter 12: Joy and Hope

1. James 1:2–3.

2. 1 Peter 1:6–8.

3. 1 Peter 1:3.

4. Isaiah 43.

Conclusion

1. Romans 8:31.

2. Deuteronomy 4:7.

3. Psalm 116:5.

www.ingramcontent.com/pod-product-compliance
Lightning Source LLC
Chambersburg PA
CBHW070657130626
46553CB00005B/1747

* 9 7 9 8 2 1 8 2 1 6 8 4 9 *